Political Will and Improving Public Schools

Previous books by the author

Curriculum on the Edge of Survival: How Schools Fail to Prepare Students for Membership in a Democracy

Curriculum on the Edge of Survival: How Schools Fail to Prepare Students for Membership in a Democracy, 2nd Edition

Taoist Lessons for Educational Leaders: Gentle Pathways to Resolving Conflicts

Political Will and Improving Public Schools

Seven Reflections for Americans to Consider

Daniel Heller

ROWMAN & LITTLEFIELD
Lanham • Boulder • New York • London

Published by Rowman & Littlefield
A wholly owned subsidiary of The Rowman & Littlefield Publishing Group, Inc.
4501 Forbes Boulevard, Suite 200, Lanham, Maryland 20706
www.rowman.com

16 Carlisle Street, London W1D 3BT, United Kingdom

Copyright © 2014 by Daniel Heller

All rights reserved. No part of this book may be reproduced in any form or by any electronic or mechanical means, including information storage and retrieval systems, without written permission from the publisher, except by a reviewer who may quote passages in a review.

British Library Cataloguing in Publication Information Available

Library of Congress Cataloging-in-Publication Data is available

ISBN 978-1-4758-0546-8 (cloth : alk. paper)
ISBN 978-1-4758-0547-5 (pbk. : alk. paper)
ISBN 978-1-4758-0548-2 (electronic)

∞™ The paper used in this publication meets the minimum requirements of American National Standard for Information Sciences Permanence of Paper for Printed Library Materials, ANSI/NISO Z39.48-1992.

Printed in the United States of America

To Nina

Contents

Preface		ix
Acknowledgments		xiii
Introduction		xv
1	Toward a Leadership Theory of Kindness and Compassion	1
2	High Schools and Wood Stoves	15
3	The Malleable High School: Meeting the Need	31
4	Teachers Are Not Professionals	43
5	Logical Leadership: Who's in Charge of School?	55
6	We Owe It to the Profession: Nurturing the Next Generation	69
7	The Product: The Purpose of Public Education	83
Conclusion		97
About the Author		101

Preface

As Socrates said, "The unexamined life is not worth living." It is in that spirit that I offer these seven reflections on American public education after serving for over thirty-three years as a teacher and administrator in the K–12 system.

When one is interviewing new teachers, a primary characteristic to look for is reflection. Does the teacher think about her practice, asking questions such as: What worked? What did not work? Was the lesson successful? What should I change? How do I know that the students learned what I had planned? What were the unanticipated consequences of the lesson? What will I have to do tomorrow as a result of what I did today?

I would be remiss, unaccountable to my profession, if I did not look back at my decades of experience and questioning and share what I have learned. Often the answers to the problems in our educational system seem so obvious. They have to do with basic trust, professionalism, and training. However, the solutions are never so simple as they seem, because we muddy the waters with self-interest, ego, power, and control issues.

People need someone or something to blame when the world does not proceed according to plan. We frequently push responsibility from ourselves and onto some other source.

Let's say we are concerned about students' cutting classes. Simple: require students to attend or face some sort of consequence, such as a reduction in grade or a detention. Problem solved. However, when we pull back the surface of the situation, we reveal a much more complex situation. Some students come from homes in which parents do not value education. Others have to work to help their families make ends meet. Still others are bored; school does not meet their needs. Some students are drawn to different diversions such as drugs or being with friends.

Typically, as stated above, our response is to ask students to conform to the ways of the school. What matters is the students' aberrant behavior, not what the school has to offer. However, as times change, we have to begin to understand that schools cannot remain stagnant in the way they deliver an education.

The time has come for the school to move as well as the student. Simply blaming the student will no longer solve the problem, if it ever did. Our student population is changing as we include more students in schools and our populace becomes more diverse. Schools cannot continue to do the same thing over and over again expecting each different child to conform to its demands.

As we glibly say, all students are individuals with specific needs, learning styles, and learning rates. Do we mean it? Do we honestly understand the implications of these beliefs?

To begin with, schools must be safe places for students to express themselves and learn freely. It is no longer sufficient to expect that students will act kindly and respectfully to one another, or for that matter, for teachers to do so. We must make treating one another humanely an explicit, active part of the curriculum.

If we are to get the best from our students, then we must provide them with a climate in which they can flourish, without fear of ridicule or bullying. Students will have to be taught to listen critically and respectfully to each other. We must allow for student mistakes, else how will any learning occur?

Too often teachers are impatient with their students. We must listen carefully to what kids are telling us and respond appropriately. We must listen carefully to what students say to each other, their parents, and other authority figures in order to get at the problem of climate. Who, if not administrators, parents, and teachers, will model positive and supportive human interactions for students? We must be aware that students are always watching us, looking to see what we do, seeking clues for correct and acceptable behavior. We are permanently on stage.

Our being role models begs the question of responsibility. Ultimately, everyone has to be responsible for his or her behavior. We cannot always look for someone else to blame. Rather than worry about blame, we should focus on repairing any damage we have done. Is it not more important to take care of the student or hurt individual first, and then try to correct the causes of the situation? At the scene of a car accident, we first take care of the victims and then try to piece together what happened, who did what.

Not only do we have to take responsibility, but we also have to allow others to take responsibility. That means we need to trust. The public needs to trust teachers to do their jobs, to make professional decisions, to mete out discipline, and to generally design the best education for each student. Parents and society in general have to resist the temptation to meddle.

This, of course, implies that teachers receive the depth of training and education required to accomplish what they set out to do. Our society should train teachers to the level of doctors and lawyers, and then give them the professional latitude to do their work. As it is, lay school boards, state and federal legislators, and parents in general loom over teachers, telling them what to do and how to do it. Teachers will never become fully professional under these circumstances, nor will society be able to hold them accountable, since their decision-making authority is so abridged.

One of the most significant aspects of a profession is the nurturing of new members of the group. As teachers, we need to do a better job at new teacher induction and inservice training. At this point, too often, we allow neophytes to sink or swim with the most challenging classes, rather than offering the necessary support to help them begin their careers successfully. Teaching assignments should become more difficult over time.

Other professions would never stand for the restrictions and oversight that educators do. We have to rethink the education system on national terms. There should be a defined body of knowledge and an extensive internship required of teachers before they begin their practice. Administrators use different skills than teachers, and consequently should receive some different training. This would suggest that master teachers be accorded the same status and salary differential that administrators now enjoy.

As schools become more responsive to students' needs, they have to become more flexible. We can no longer stick to strict schedules that do not accommodate any but traditional students. We cannot hold back more talented students, nor restrict the time slower students need to complete work. School systems will have to be honestly competency based, with the variable being time, not mastery.

The educational delivery system needs to deliver a consistent education, but not necessarily in a consistent way. For instance, what one student might learn through independent study another might need twelve months of instruction to master. Different students learn at different times of the day, at different times of the year.

So we need to be able to treat our students like patients, developing a plan to optimize each one's learning. This will mean a school with many options for professionals to call upon. We cannot afford to lose any student's potential contribution to our society.

Summer schools, afterschool programs, correspondence courses, and independent studies all come into play. Hopefully schools will develop creative ways to involve the community in the educations of many students as well.

At the same time, we need to be completely clear about the purpose of education. Why do we teach what we do? What is the result of a good public education supposed to be? Are we about preparation for college and the workplace only? What about the ability to appreciate and live the good life? Is there a spiritual component to education? Is education really the great leveler, allowing all members of a democratic society to participate fully in that society?

What ties these chapters together is the concept of political will. I think we can develop new systems to correct the more blatant problems in public education, but do we have the will to implement them? As a given, change is never easy. However, the changes here are particularly uncomfortable. People will play new roles and have to learn new skills and build new relationships. Educators and the community will have to shift attitudes of blame and trust. Teachers and administrators will have to live up to the requirements of being professionals, both in terms of training and practice.

Some people will have to give up power, or at the very least share it with others. Lines of communication and command will change. Each player in the system will have to see the problems as bigger than themselves, and thus be willing to sacrifice the way things are to the way things could be. There will be sacrifice.

If education were a manufacturing operation, we would shut down and retool. Are we at that point? Have we come to a time when we have applied so many patches to schools that we are now putting patches on patches? How do we shut down so that we can rebuild?

As one can see, to rethink education, perhaps even to rebuild it from the ground up, will take tremendous resources, efforts, selflessness, and will. The question remains, as reflected in each of these chapters, to examine whether or not we mean what we say. Or will the wealthy slip away into independent schools of privilege while the public schools become ever more challenging? I cannot predict the outcome. What I can do is point out what I have learned from serving, observing, and reflecting on my own practice as an educator, and the potential dangers ahead.

This book is not intended as a set of complaints about public education. It is hopefully not merely an idealistic but impossible and unpractical vision. It is an attempt to understand the issues we as a country face with respect to how we educate our populace. It is a kind of parsing of the situation in a way meant to be accessible to the layperson and professional educator alike. My goal is to start a process of thinking and reflecting that may lead to creative and substantive solutions for education. If the chapters in this book make the reader think about and reflect on the educational experience in this country, then I will have done my job.

Acknowledgments

I want to thank Nina, Ben, Pam, Anthony, and Namiah for their continued love and support. Thanks to Andy Platt, Walter Cramer, and Pam Bullock for their generous contributions to this project. I am grateful to the Association of Supervision and Curriculum Development and the Association of Black Psychologists for permission to use their publications. And finally, my appreciation goes to Socrates and HPR.

Introduction

The chapters in this book deal with situations or issues in public education that we need to address. While some of these situations seem clear and almost obvious, making the necessary changes and admitting the truth to ourselves is not necessarily going to happen easily.

The suggestions for education made here will require that Americans admit certain flaws in the system, some of which involve their own actions and attitudes. They will also have to be willing to make sacrifices for the larger good, such as allowing shifts in power and control. In other words, these changes will require political will, patience, and dedication if they are to be successful.

There are many ideas for fixing our schools. They all demand a kind of faith, a promise to withhold judgment for a while until the new strategies are fully tested to decide whether or not they are effective. People can be impatient, wanting instant answers. They can also want assurance of success before ever agreeing to allow a change to happen.

These attitudes block experimentation and the attempt at change and improvement. Everyone will have to sacrifice, to take a risk, if we are to make real changes in the education system. All constituencies (students, teachers, administrators, parents, community members, institutions of higher education, teacher-preparation programs, and unions) should be at the table. What they should be working toward is not their individual agendas or preservation, but the delivery of the best education possible to our youth.

The first chapter discusses the need to teach kindness in the schools. This is not to say that teachers are not kind or caring about their students. They most certainly are. However, people are not naturally kind, and such behavior should be modeled explicitly by adults. We must give students the tools to be empathic, respectful, and mutually supportive.

Without kindness, the school atmosphere ceases to be conducive to learning. Students may be afraid of bullies. They may even be afraid of harsh adults. People will not speak openly and offer their ideas if they worry about being mocked by others. Schools can reinforce the concept of a respectful, supportive, open forum within their walls, thus allowing the free flow of ideas.

The second chapter addresses the issue of high-school dropouts. How we count them does not matter. What does is that there are dropouts at all. As schools become increasingly inclusive, they cannot afford to rely on old structures and strategies working for all populations. We know that students learn in different ways and at different rates.

This chapter offers numerous variations of how we deliver an acceptable education to high-school students. There is no point in taking students who are not doing well once again through the system in which they did poorly. Instead, the schools must find educational means adapted to the various types of students who come through their doorways.

To create these variations, we will need to rethink the way schools do business. Schedules, roles, materials, teaching methodology, classrooms, and student activity are all variables we should consider in reshaping high school. Of course, such a goal will demand that everyone involved be flexible and willing to take on new roles and power relationships. This will not be an easy path, but if people can withhold judgment long enough, even over a period of years, change is possible.

Does learning have to take place in a classroom? Does it have to happen in group situations? Can community members offer their expertise to students for credit? Can a job possibly count as an educational experience leading to credit toward graduation? We need to ask these and other questions in order to develop more creative ways in which to offer a meaningful education to all of our students.

The third chapter looks at the structure of the American high school. With all of the innovation happening, most high schools still look more or less the same as they did more than fifty years ago. The school is a series of rooms in which individual teachers deliver instruction to groups of students in specific topics in discreet amounts of time.

If we want to offer education in various ways, as discussed in chapter 2, then we will have to rethink the very structural elements of the high school: schedules, roles, power relationships. The schools will need the flexibility necessary to fit to the students rather than demanding that students fit to the schools. Teachers and schools will have to have the independent authority to deliver instruction to students in the best manner as determined through their professional training.

Summer school could allow students to accelerate their programs or extend their studies if they need more time to complete their work. This kind of flexibility would allow for a true standards-based program, one in which meeting the standard, and not seat time, determined a student's progress. There would be no grade levels in such a system, only progress made toward standards. Any one class could hold students of various ages and abilities. Students gifted in an area could move more quickly through the material than others who are not as gifted. Students could find their own comfort levels.

The school would be open all year round, and from 7:00 a.m. to 10:00 p.m. to accommodate all students, including adults and those with full-time jobs. Students could even choose what time of year they would take vacation, not necessarily the summer only. Imagine the willpower necessary to change high schools like this. It can be done, but only if we have the patience to weather setbacks, criticism, political fallout, and all the rest that comes with major change.

The fourth chapter may be the most controversial. It questions the status of teachers and educators in general as professionals. Although this sounds like a criticism of teachers, it is actually a criticism of the system in general. When the job of a teacher is measured against the characteristics of a profession, it definitely falls short.

For instance, teachers do not enjoy the autonomy of most professionals. There are no common standards for entering teaching. Teachers have little control over who becomes a new teacher. They are controlled by a lay board that has direct access to them. State and federal governments tell teachers what to do, constantly burdening them with more and more responsibilities.

Much of the situation is based on a lack of trust by the public that teachers will do a good job. Some of this may be justified by poor teacher-preparation programs. Another source of this situation is the control the community has over teachers. This makes every citizen a boss, so to speak, of the teachers. These bosses want to exercise their power, and they do. We do not question our doctors, lawyers, and accountants the way we second-guess teachers. In addition, everyone has easy access to teachers to list their grievances.

Teachers have unions. This sets up an immediate conflict. Are they blue collar employees or are they white collar? How can a professional have defined hours, little flexibility, and minimal authority over his or her own work? Once again, this grows out of years of mistrust so that teachers feel they need the protections unions and contracts afford. At the same time, this situation holds them back from becoming the professionals they should be.

The fifth chapter concerns itself with school governance, a topic touched on above. Who calls the shots in education? Chapter 5 suggests that schools use a system modeled after the way in which hospitals are run. There could be two strands of governance, one administrative, and one professional.

The administrative strand would take care of day-to-day operations: plant management, discipline, contracts, organization. The professional strand would look after professional matters: supervision of instruction, curriculum development, staffing, professional development. There would be a principal and a chief of staff to run the school together, each specializing in one aspect of the institution. They would work together on issues such as the budget, and they would both answer to the board.

This system would honor the different roles needed to direct a successful school. The job of the principal as it now stands is untenable. Building and grounds alone could be a full-time position. At the same time, teachers would have increased professional status, being allowed to make decisions about professional matters. One can only imagine how difficult this change would be, since it asks individuals to give up specific powers, and others to take on increased responsibilities. Again, one has to ask if we as a nation have the will to do this.

The sixth chapter discusses the role of professionals in gatekeeping and supporting new members. In other words, current members of the group have a significant say in who is ready to enter their ranks. This can be problematic for many reasons, as mentioned above. But what teachers can do immediately is to take care of new members of the profession. Too often new teachers are given the most difficult classes and then left to sink or swim on their own.

There are more and more mentoring programs emerging, which is a good sign. There is more to do, however. Teacher-preparation programs and public schools must forge strong relationships to develop programs together. They should be responsible for the training of preservice teachers and the continued support of new teachers in the classroom full time.

There should be comprehensive mentoring programs, with master teachers being trained as mentors. Schools of higher education could continue to offer courses for the new teacher to help with the adjustment to actual work as a teacher. In fact, such courses could be developed by higher education and the schools together, and then taught by a member of the school system, offering graduate credit.

As a profession, teachers deserve a greater say in the preparation of new teachers, and they owe those new members the support necessary to allow them to be successful. Schools use outside people for professional development when all the time they have extensive untapped resources within their own faculties. We should allow the experienced teachers to share their knowledge and expertise with those new to teaching.

Finally, the last chapter discusses the purposes of education. At first blush, the answer seems to be obvious, and perhaps it is in the ideal. However, there are a number of possible purposes for education, including preparing students to be active, productive members of a democratic society, creating whole human beings, preparing students for the work force, preparing students for postsecondary education, and passing on the culture and values of society. A more negative purpose may be to maintain power and economic advantages for those already wealthy and powerful.

Americans must ask themselves what they want of their education system. What is their goal for their children? What is their goal for all Americans? These are powerful questions, the answers to which could determine the future course of our nation.

Few people will deny that our public education system has flaws. The controversy comes when we try to define those flaws and develop strategies for correcting them. We will have to be painfully honest with ourselves and put aside personal agendas. The real purpose of these changes is to maximize the experience of all students.

Choosing one aspect of education to work on will be challenging. As the chapters in this book indicate, the various issues in schools are interrelated to the point where one must talk about several of them at once at any given time. Roles, resources, strategies, structures, and governance all inform each other. Reformers will have to keep the whole picture in mind as they try to work on a piece of the puzzle.

As this book shows over and over again, we will need tremendous political and ethical will to move forward. People will have to be ready to see the world differently and do things differently from the way things have always been done. They will need to accept changing roles and power differentials. They will have to re-vision public education, teacher preparation, and school governance.

The final question is: Do we have the courage to make the hard choices and changes, do we have the honesty, do we have the patience and will to make America's public schools what they should be?

NOTE: To avoid awkward constructions such as "her or she" or "he/she" I have used the female pronoun at times and the male pronoun at times. My intent is to simplify the writing without offending anyone.

ONE
Toward a Leadership Theory of Kindness and Compassion

THE MISSING PIECES

What do aspiring principals learn in their preparation programs? What do in-service principals learn in the workshops, programs, and courses they take? Obviously, they study many leadership topics including situational leadership, clinical supervision, evaluation of personnel, Gantt charts, empowerment, and all the laws one needs to follow to dismiss a teacher.

Some supervisors explain to principals that there are times when they should know how to "put their knee in someone's back," and not to let "them" have too much information. Some advise that principals should never ask questions they do not already know the answers to.

Principals learn to conduct force-field analyses, create a critical mass, and even make a group decision. They take workshops that discuss bottom lines, flattening organizations, being mean and lean, and generally revering the model provided by the business sector. Leaders may have to learn the ins and outs of shared governance. Add to all this the intricacies of building and understanding complex budgets. Just think about managing a large physical plant.

Rarely, if ever, does one hear in the context of leadership the words "kindness" and "compassion." Education is personal, founded on positive relationships. Principals cannot always see education as a production process with a quantifiable conclusion. It is not a competitive process. It is a people process, founded upon human interactions and positive relationships.

Rather than looking at production models, power models, and business models, school leaders should be looking in some other directions that incorporate kindness and compassion. Sometimes school personnel see discussions of kindness as insulting. Of course, they think, they are kind people. However, there is a need to model kindness overtly, as an example for teachers and students. This cannot be overstated.

Two relevant areas for all educators to understand are research on brain-based activity and the wisdom of the ancient Far East. The former reveals in a painfully empirical manner the actual physical and psychological harm that a lack of kindness and compassion can do. The latter intuits the incredible power that can result from their use.

If educators treated students the way they too often treat one another as professionals, they would be reprimanded for their behaviors. Best practice counsels teachers to be patient with students. They learn to preserve students' dignity and sense of self-esteem. They learn to use differentiated instruction to reflect the fact that each student is an individual. Shouldn't this attention to the individual extend then to staff interactions in the same way? Should they not be modeling these behaviors?

This can be more difficult than it at first appears. Daily pressure, negative experiences, and the need at times for an immediate response can all affect the way people treat one another. Patience is the key. If school personnel can learn to be mindful of their immediate reactions and pause before acting on them, then they will have a better chance of acting thoughtfully and without assumptions. People know what to do. However, it takes effort to maintain compassion and kindness in the face of life's challenges.

A SELF-FULFILLING PROPHECY

People tend to see confrontations or conflicts in terms of right and wrong, winners and losers. The world becomes a zero-sum game. They can be so convinced of this reality that they make their beliefs come true by anticipating the results of an incident so strongly that they ignore what is actually happening. People create the self-fulfilling prophecy of conflict and punishment.

Imagine the situation of the principal of a middle school where a young man is sent to the office for his behavior. Before the principal encounters the student, she thinks of Sun Tzu's book, *The Art of War*, written in China two thousand years ago. Sun Tzu directs his words, for the most part, at what generals need to know in order to lead successful campaigns.

Sun Tzu

Although Sun Tzu wrote of commanding armies and entering into battle, his words have relevance for the educational leader. At the base of the philosopher's ideas is the resolution of conflict with as little destruction, psychologically or physically, as is possible. In a metaphorical sense, all conflicts are battles, and opposite sides are armies or enemies.

In writing of the "Strategy of Attack," Sun Tzu said,

> Therefore, one hundred victories in one hundred
> battles is not the most skillful.
> Subduing the other's military without battle is
> most skillful. (Sun Tzu 2001, 9)

In other words, the best battle is the one that one does not fight. How can school personnel resolve differences without entering into open conflict?

The Blurted-Out Comments

The young man mentioned above has a problem of blurting out his thoughts or answers out of turn. After a while, this behavior begins to bother the teacher a great deal. The teacher, exasperated at the constant interruptions, finally sends the student to the office.

He enters angry, practically in tears, and ready for the system to beat him down. He has already decided how the situation will play out. He has no faith that the principal will honestly listen to and appreciate his side of the story. Thus, the principal's job is not to live down to the student's expectations, to corroborate his negative vision of reality.

What follows is a possible dialogue between the principal and the student. (P = principal, S = student).

P: Come in. Sit down. Why are you here?

S: Now you are going to give me a detention or send me home.

P: Did I say anything about sending you home or detentions?

S: That's what you are going to do.

P: Why are you here?

S: Because the teacher said that I was interrupting class by speaking out of turn.

P: Were you?

S: Now you are just going to punish me and I didn't do anything.

P: Did you speak out of turn?

S: I can't help it. I always say what is in my head. I told you I would be in trouble.

P: Did I say you were in trouble?

S: Well, you are going to give me a detention.

P: Why do you blurt things out of turn?

S: I didn't do anything.

P: Did I say you did anything? I asked you why you speak out of turn.

S: Well, the words pop up in my head, and then after a second or two they just come out.

P: Do you think that during those few seconds you could catch yourself and count to ten?

S: Why should I when you are just going to punish me?

P: Did I say I was going to punish you? I simply asked if you could count to ten before saying what is in your head.

S: But I didn't do anything.

P: Did I say that you did anything? I asked you if you could count to ten and stop yourself from blurting out the words in your head.

S: I guess so.

P: So you can do that?

S: Yeah.

P: OK, then next time, please count to ten before you speak out of turn. Now return to class.

The principal refused to play into bigger versus smaller or powerful versus weak. She had no intention of entering into a power struggle. Instead, she treated the student as an intelligent, thinking being. The principal did not insult him, nor did she overwhelm him. Unfortunately, the system had already conditioned him to expect the worst, but the principal would not buy into that. For her, there was a problem to resolve, with respect and kindness.

Remaining compassionate and kind is not always easy. People test each other every day, and the principal's or teacher's job is to prove them wrong, to show them that the world does not have to be the negative and painful reality that they are so sure that it is, thus breaking the cycle of a worldview they are about to repeat and confirm.

TAKING WHOLE

Punishing this student would have been easy, and the principal would have won the battle because her forces were clearly superior. She also would have confirmed his negative beliefs and destroyed the possibility of an emerging relationship.

That time, the teacher got what she wanted—for the student to understand that he should pause before he decided to speak—and she did not have to crush her "enemy" in the process. No one ever sent him to the office for that offense again. Sun Tzu calls this "taking whole."

Taking whole means to win the battle without destroying the enemy. In other words, can one maintain everyone's dignity and integrity in the process? In this way, one will not have further alienated the other and destroyed any possibility of a positive relationship. One needs to deal with opponents compassionately. Winning at the cost of bitterness and mistrust may not be a victory at all, at best a temporary cessation of hostilities.

The Bitter Teacher

Imagine a principal who supervises a difficult teacher. The teacher is a bitter complainer, often coming to the office with a host of issues. At first, the principal would try to engage him in conversation, trying to solve the problems which he elaborated. This never worked, because he had an answer for every suggestion the principal made, and there was no end to the depressing conversation. Perhaps, thought the administrator, all the teacher wanted was for someone to listen, to lend a compassionate ear.

From then on, the conversations proceeded more positively. The principal would not say anything, but just listen to the teacher actively and intently. When the teacher was done, he would usually leave after exchanging a few closing pleasantries. He did not want advice. He wanted someone to care.

By merely listening the principal could help relieve the teacher's suffering. The administrator had seen a conflict where there was none, and finally responded appropriately. She did not have to create the reality she assumed. Instead she withheld judgment and listened. The principal did not have to insert her ego into the situation.

HUMILITY

Sun Tzu writes of the general,

> And so he advances yet does not seek fame.
> He retreats yet does not avoid blame.
> He seeks only to preserve the people (Sun Tzu 2001, 43).

Being an educator or educational leader is not about climbing career ladders. It is about service. And service is about listening to others, caring about and for them, and quietly going about doing one's job. This is an area of leadership where education can go awry, particularly with respect to emulating the business model.

Schools are not in the same kind of competition as businesses. Society cannot afford to see learning as a commodity that can be simply measured. It cannot force people to learn or legislate that students will be at a certain level of achievement after a defined amount of time.

Sure, society has moved into an era that demands that we be the best in our individual schools to attract students who have choices, but being best does not necessarily mean being the toughest or the one with the highest test scores. It may very well mean just the opposite, holding high standards, but at the same time helping individuals, both students and staff, to reach them through our being supportive and kind. Along with high test scores, one should consider the overall qualitative characteristics of an institution.

Lao Tzu, the author of the *Tao Te Ching* (*Book of the Way*), also had much to say about the most valuable characteristics of the good leader. Sometime in China around the sixth century BC, he wrote,

> All streams flow to the sea
> because it is lower than they are.
> Humility gives it its power. (Lao Tzu 1989, 66)

He also wrote,

> I have just three things to teach:
> simplicity, patience, compassion.
> These are your greatest treasures.
> Simple in actions and in thoughts,
> you return to the source of being.
> Patient with both friends and enemies,
> you accord with the way things are.
> Compassionate toward yourself,
> You reconcile all beings in the world. (Lao Tzu 1989, 67)

Humility, patience, compassion, simplicity—these are at the core of good leadership. This in no way implies weakness. One must make difficult decisions; one must insist on certain levels of performance. The paradox, however, is that these kinds of goals can be accomplished without an overpowering leadership based on ego, harsh orders, or aggressive confrontation.

CARING VS. CONTROL

Ego is about competition, power, mastery, and control. Education should be about helping students become humane, caring individuals, capable of dealing with the complex issues the world presents. Educators can model humane behavior for their students (by demonstrating it through interactions with peers) without sacrificing standards of learning or behavior.

As Lao Tzu wrote,

> Nothing in the world
> is as soft and yielding as water.
> Yet for dissolving the hard and inflexible,
> nothing can surpass it.
>
> The soft overcomes the hard;
> the gentle overcomes the rigid.
> Everyone knows this is true,
> but few can put it into practice. (Lao Tzu 1989, 78)

A leader can be rigid, holding strictly to the contract. There are no excuses for being late. No one can leave early. All hours must be accounted for. The results of such leadership are rigidity and conflict. One can be sure that there will be grievances every time the leader steps out of contractual line even the slightest bit. One can be sure that when the principal asks for a favor, such as staying five extra minutes to finish some work, the answer will be no.

WORKING GENTLY

Certainly, one can get results with harsh orders, a winner/loser mentality, and holding a hard line. However, working gently but persistently with people ultimately effects a more productive impression. One can force the world into the desired shape, just like destroying a mountain with explosives. Or, like water, one can gently, over time, shape the world to one's wishes. The latter method does not destroy, but rather it redefines. The rigid eventually break, while the persistent and flexible, over time, survive.

Without compassion and kindness, allowing for people's individual needs, the system becomes mechanical and unyielding. Sometimes people just need some time to collect themselves after days of challenging work. People can have personal problems that one must acknowledge. Professionals can disagree, but they can do so with respect and interest in each other's positions.

> If the country is governed with tolerance,
> the people are comfortable and honest.
> If a country is governed with repression,

the people are depressed and crafty. (Lau Tzu 1988 58)

People do not have to be depressed and crafty. They are so in response to the environment in which they find themselves. If they have no need of these characteristics because they work in a world of tolerance and openness, then they will develop honesty in an environment of comfort. This latter condition is certainly more conducive to a productive, smooth-running operation than not. Remaining flexible and not simply responding automatically to a situation is vital to success.

PRIORITIES

Often administrators hold the belief that their priorities should be students first, program second, and teachers third. Certainly, if at all possible, students should always come first. However, the order of the second and third priorities is not so simple, and a rigid application of this advice may not always be warranted.

Consider the case of a teacher who came to the principal to talk privately. Once in the office, he explained that he and his wife were under a great deal of stress, and that this was affecting their marriage. The couple needed some time to be together away from their jobs, just a day or two. The teacher began to cry. At that moment, the administrator's first order of concern was not the program, but the pain of the human being sitting across from her. She could not sacrifice her humanity to "the program" at that point. Being kind and compassionate means being flexible according to the demands of the situation.

Yes, finding a suitable substitute would be difficult, especially on short notice. Yes, this would mean a temporary dip in the quality of the program. But ultimately the decision was simply to have the teacher call in sick for a couple of days, and the principal would somehow cover the gap.

This example does not qualify as tough leadership. However, it does qualify as humane and therefore intelligent leadership. By not assisting this person in need, the quality of instruction and thus the program would surely have, in the long run, deteriorated as the teacher's life situation became more stressful.

By helping him to make the needed life adjustments, the principal knew that she would save a fine teacher and gain his loyalty in the bargain. In addition, she was contributing to an overall climate of caring, and in an indirect way modeling this for students and other professionals.

When principals treat teachers with compassion, those teachers will be much more willing to put in extra hours as needed, to be there for others in crisis situations covering classes, and generally willing to do what needs to be done at any given time. In other words, by putting teachers before program in certain situations, the principal actually strengthens the program and her base of support.

Kindness and compassion are powerful forces for change, team building, loyalty, cooperation, and strength. They are key characteristics of successful administrations, which should be about nurturing successful schools, not about developing a traditional power hierarchy with the principal at the top. Educational leadership is not about personal career climbing, personal importance, or empire building. It is about creating humane systems in which professionals and students can take risks in order to grow and learn without fear, undue stress, or too much anxiety.

THE DANGERS OF STRESS

Stress kills. The brain research of the last thirty years shows this to be true. By driving people with pressure and a lack of kindness and compassion, we keep up the stress. While this may garner short-term results, in the long term it is costly. Patricia Wolfe, in her book *Brain Matters*, tells us that

> The stress response was designed for life in caves, but we don't live there anymore. The contemporary human brain doesn't distinguish between actual physical danger and psychological danger; it sets the same psychological chain of events in motion in either case. Having your blood pressure go up, blood clotting elements released in your bloodstream, and your immune system suppressed is fine if you are faced with a cave bear. But it isn't particularly helpful when someone pulls into a parking space you thought was yours. The stress response, with its release of cortisol and epinephrine, was designed to last a relatively short time, until you outran the bear or became its dinner. In contemporary life, however, we often extend the response by talking about the stressful event, reliving it, or worrying that it will happen again. We have a tendency to keep ourselves in a chronic, prolonged fight-or-flight state, with potentially negative consequences. High concentrations of cortisol over a long period of time can provoke hippocampal deterioration and cognitive decline. With prolonged stress, the immune system is compromised, increasing the risk of illness, acceleration of disease, and retardation of growth. (Wolfe 2001, 110)

One may find oneself in a state of continuous stress because of the atmosphere of the workplace. A student is subject to continuous stress due to bullying or an unnecessarily authoritarian teacher. Stress for such a duration, as seen above, can have deleterious effects.

Beside those already mentioned, there are several additional dangers. Those increased clotting elements released into the bloodstream increase the risk of heart attack. By shifting blood from the digestive system to the large muscle groups, food may not be processed as it should. Blood pressure rises. The hippocampal damage can result in permanent memory impairment.

MYTHS ABOUT KINDNESS AND COMPASSION

The antidote to stress is kindness and compassion. There are a number of myths or paradoxes about kindness and compassion in leadership positions. An examination of them can be illuminating of one's leadership style and effectiveness.

1. *Kindness is weakness, and sternness is strength.* Kindness is, in fact, a great strength. Through kindness one wins people over, takes whole, as Sun Tzu said. Kindness begets allies and avoids having people work out of fear. Eventually, fear breeds unhappiness and disease, while kindness develops a healthy trust and loyalty.
2. *There is no place for emotion. Emotion clouds thinking.* Quite the contrary. Brain research tells us that "emotion is very important to the educative process because it drives attention, which drives learning and memory (Sylwester 1995, 72). In fact, what would be a better way to get the best from people than to let them know that you care about them? Of course, one cannot make difficult decisions based solely on emotion. Sometimes one has to make unpopular choices, or ones that leave certain people disappointed, for the welfare of the group.

    Over time, if someone is not working out well, a leader will probably have to counsel that person out of the workplace. However, even this can be done with kindness. People will respect you more if they know that you are making decisions in a compassionate and supportive way, even if the ultimate results are painful.
3. *A leader should demand the best of people.* Or should one *expect the best* from others? Expectation implies trust and confidence. Demands imply that without it, people's natural laziness would take over. Why not go with the positive approach? This has the added benefit of reducing stress.
4. *There is no time or space for listening to personal problems.* This is simply short-sighted. Principals are dealing with human beings. Maslow's hierarchy of needs suggests that people are not going to function at high levels until their basic needs are met. A few minutes of empathic listening can save a great deal of anguish and unproductive time.

    A standard belief is that employees' bringing personal problems to work is unprofessional. However, we cannot expect people to compartmentalize their lives absolutely, to ignore emotional stress. "It's impossible to separate emotion from the important activities of life. Don't even try" (Sylwester 1995, 75). Principals need to deal

with the whole person, just as teachers are instructed to deal with the whole student. Students under emotional stress cannot function effectively. Neither can the staff.
5. *Caring about employees should be second to caring about the institution.* The problem with this concept is that it misses the fundamental truth that the institution is comprised of people. If your head hurts, you probably do not perform at your best until you deal with the pain. So too, an employee in pain will have a ripple effect on the functioning of the whole system.
6. *Don't use the carrot; use the stick.* By this time, one should see the obvious benefit in a system of rewards as opposed to one of punishments. One only has to think of the punitive nature of the No Child Left Behind Act to understand how a system of negative sanctions is oppressive and uninspiring. Pride, confidence, recognition, and actual physical rewards create an atmosphere of caring and support. The stick, like demands, creates stress and mistrust. Rewards are like expectations. They recognize and encourage good work.
7. *Keep relationships impersonal. Personal relationships are dangerous and unprofessional.* All good teaching begins with positive relationships between teachers and students. Why should this be any different for other groups of people working together? Personal relationships reveal our human fallibility to one another. This allows us to be vulnerable and make mistakes. One knows that the other understands that this is a part of our being human. We can come to one another honestly and ask for help without fear of being seen as weak or unintelligent.

Personal relationships inspire loyalty and mutual support. Impersonality leaves people on the level of functional machine parts, inevitably leading to a sense of spiritlessness on the job, a feeling of going through the motions only. This is not to say that one should not maintain a sense of professional objectivity to avoid favoritism or making a decision on the basis of pure emotion.

Thich Nhat Hanh

The Vietnamese Buddhist monk Thich Nhat Hanh had this to say about the intelligence of compassionate action:

> Understanding and compassion are very powerful sources of energy. They are the opposite of stupidity and passivity. If you think that compassion is passive, weak, or cowardly, then you don't know what real compassion or understanding is. If you think that compassionate people do not resist and challenge injustice, you are wrong. They are warriors, heroes, and heroines who have gained many victories. When you act with compassion, with non-violence . . . you have to be very strong.

> Compassion grows constantly inside of you, and you can succeed in your fight against injustice. Mahatma Gandhi was just one person. He did not have any bombs, and guns, or any political party. He acted simply on the . . . strength of compassion, not on the basis of anger. (Hahn 2001, 128)

Kindness and compassion are two missing elements of administrators' training. We must then seek these forces within ourselves to maximize our strength and productivity. Only in this way will we reach our potential as human beings, and help others to reach theirs.

Part of educator training could be an examination of the soft skills, such as relationship building. While most people know how to treat others, increasing mindfulness will help individuals avoid the subtle missteps in communication that can be so hurtful. While this is on one level a very simple idea, in reality it can be difficult to implement.

Individuals are loath to admit weakness in this area. They are subject to all kinds of pressures working against their being kind and compassionate. By practicing mindfulness through actual courses and workshops, educators can become more automatic in their dealing with others with kindness and respect.

Education is a totally human enterprise about the development of children into healthy, productive members of society. Certainly, this can only be advanced through an atmosphere of kindness and compassion.

Hopefully, those students will carry that sprit out into the world with them.

Jewel

The popular singer Jewel recorded a song called "Hands" on the Atlantic label in 1998. One stanza stands out with respect to this discussion.

> My hands are small I know
> But they're not yours they are my own
> Not yours they are my own
> And we are never broken
> In the end only kindness matters
> In the end only kindness matters. (Jewel and Leonard 1998)

ESSENTIALS TO REMEMBER

Administrator preparation programs do not often include soft skills such as building personal relationships, using kindness, and being compassionate.

The ancient wisdom of the Far East teaches a great deal about humane leadership. Educators do not have to see confrontations as win/lose situations. There can be compromise, dignity, and respect. Avoiding a battle can be more powerful than winning it.

Leaders do not have to live down to negative institutional expectations. Every infraction does not have to lead to punishment. Every disagreement does not have to lead to winners and losers. Taking whole, or avoiding the total destruction of an opponent, will allow that opponent to maintain his or her dignity and be available as a colleague and ally in the future. Leave people a way out to save face.

Simplicity, patience, and compassion are key characteristics of leadership. Compassion begets compassion, loyalty, and esprit de corps. It can be a powerful force for positive change and the development of positive relationships.

Leaders need to lead with intelligence and kindness, not with ego. There is little room for rigidity. One can care about people instead of trying to control them. Working gently garners results. Learning is not a commodity, and education is not a business.

Stress is physically and psychologically damaging. It can literally kill a person as well as immobilize him or her. It can cause physical damage to the brain. Stress begets an atmosphere of fear, resentment, and anger. This is no way to build a school.

Kindness is not weakness. There is room for kindness and respect. Emotions are real and need to be recognized and integrated into dealing with people. Leading by expectation is a better way of administering than leading by demand. There needs to be time for accepting and working with personal problems.

Education is a humane enterprise.

REFERENCES

Hahn, Thich Nhat. (2001). *Anger: Wisdom for Cooling the Flames.* New York: Penguin.
Jewel, and Patrick Leonard. (1998). *Hands.* Atlantic.
Lao Tzu. (1989). *Tao Te Ching,* trans. Stephan Mitchell. New York: Harper and Row.
Sun Tzu. (2001). *The Art of War, a New Translation,* trans. Denma Translation Group. Boston and London: Shambhala.
Sylwester, Robert. (1995). *A Celebration of Neurons: An Educator's Guide to the Human Brain.* Alexandria, VA: Association for Supervision and Curriculum Development.
Wolfe, Patricia. (2001). *Brain Matters: Translating Research into Classroom Practice.* Alexandria, VA: Association for Supervision and Curriculum Development.

TWO
High Schools and Wood Stoves

Contemporary wood-burning stoves have baffle systems that recirculate the smoke back through the fire chamber. By so doing, unburned particles and gases burn more completely; there is greater combustion. Consequently, the exhaust that the stove ultimately releases into the air is cleaner and less toxic than it would have been otherwise. Combustion is finished rather than being only partial.

High schools also need a process by which unfinished students are recirculated through the teaching-learning system. We call these students dropouts, and they threaten to leave the school before their education is completed. Schools need to capture them to complete their education. The difference, though, is that the school cannot put them through the same process from which they fled, but accommodate the process to their distinct situations, learning needs, and interests.

There are many programs designed to address this situation, but they necessitate change. The question is whether or not schools have the political will and professional courage to learn alternative ways for delivering education and then making the necessary adjustments to day-to-day operation, necessarily leaving current comfort zones behind.

There are various systems for counting dropouts from a particular school or in a specified region. At times, individuals argue over which methodology is most accurate (Zubrzycki 2012, 1, 12). This is a good example of missing the forest for the trees. How we count dropouts is interesting, but the real issue is that we have dropouts at all. Energy would be better spent on the problem itself. Can we develop a system for catching these students before they leave the school incomplete?

FREEDOM AND CONNECTION

Several issues are worthy of exploration. First, how can we engage all students in their educations, particularly in high school? Second, how do we give students freedom to experiment while maintaining the connection to the school? For instance, if a student is working in an internship for a semester, can we institute characteristics of that internship that require the student to have regular involvement with the school? Once the educational institution loses direct contact with a student, it has less and less chance of bringing that student back into the regular program.

Tutoring

Much can be done with tutoring. Some schools have a tutoring center, where students can get help throughout the day. There are also before and after school tutors. These tutoring options would have to be staffed in some way, and that may include hiring generalist tutors to supplement discipline-specific tutors, such as math or science teachers.

Tutoring can keep a struggling student from turning away from school. Tutors can also provide the individual attention some students need to believe that there are caring adults in the building. Thus, students are rerouted through a nontraditional approach to education that helps them complete their work.

Tutoring involves personnel and time. Schools could offer tutoring as one teacher duty instead of cafeteria duty or study hall. Paraprofessionals, school resource officers, volunteers, and some teachers could staff these nonprofessional duties. By using teachers as tutors, the schools make better use of professional time, which is an in-kind budget advantage.

The cost of tutors is diminished by using adults other than teachers in other management roles, although requirements that tutors be highly qualified may also increase the expense of the project. Society will have to weigh the cost of dropouts (joblessness, crime, welfare) against the cost of keeping students in school.

One inventive school offered two two-period tutoring sessions, one in the morning, and one after school. The program actually allowed some students to attend one of these sessions as their entire school day. Once again, this allowed the school to maintain contact and a relationship with students. The students could enjoy the benefits of connection with caring adults while working independently.

Keeping students connected to the school is absolutely crucial. That is the reason to allow a student to attend a tutoring session and then go to work or whatever outside commitment the student may have. During tutoring, students can work on basic skills in language arts, math, science, and social studies. If possible, the student should earn some general graduation credit for completing a semester of tutoring.

A program such as this one allows the school to remain a part of the students' lives, with the eventual hope that they will integrate back into the regular program. As already mentioned, once a student leaves, returning to school is not likely. Schools have to stay in touch with their struggling students.

School boards, administrators, teachers, and parents may have to break some rules or even create new ones if they are to recast the system into something different. Issues of certification, pay, and contractual obligations all need to be considered, and hopefully in such a way as not to block a potentially good idea. If students truly come first, then boards and unions will come to terms with new approaches. This is already happening in schools with desperate budget situations.

Ideally, students should have access to tutors throughout the day. This might be managed by making tutoring a teacher duty. Rather than watch student lunches, watch bathrooms, and watch hallways, teachers could and should be using their time in professional activities. Schools now often have school safety officers and paraprofessionals who can help supervise unstructured time.

The program would not demand that all teachers participate. There may remain study halls and such, which will take some teachers' time. However, tutoring throughout the day allows students easier access to the help they may need to see their educations as viable.

There also remains the possibility of tutoring for some specific students through the Special Education program. This option, of course, entails all of the regulations around eligibility and placement that the law requires. However, pull-out programs are becoming increasingly unpopular, so this type of tutoring may not be available everywhere. We need to see this type of tutoring as supplemental in nature. Along these lines, a school could also look to Title I for additional student support. Response to Intervention (RTI), inclusion, and coteaching all offer potential solutions for the student who is struggling.

Tutoring during the day would be for academic support in specific academic disciplines. This is not the same as the morning and afternoon tutoring sessions described above. Those would more likely accommodate students who are at high risk of dropping out, students who are disillusioned with the educational system. Tutoring during the day would help to keep students from getting to that point in their attitude toward education.

All tutoring helps students stay in school. For the majority, these supports allow students to be successful. For the disenchanted, these services may be the only way certain students can survive in difficult times.

The two most significant factors in a tutoring process are accessibility and relevance. For the at-risk students, one also has to be aware of social and emotional issues. The tutor needs to form bonds with these kids, making the tutoring room a safe place to be. There is an element of counseling here, as there is in all good teaching. Relationships are often at the core of successful teaching. These students can be especially needy. In fact, meeting these social and emotional needs may be the primary reason some students attend tutoring sessions at all.

Tutoring is an offer of help and hope to students who are struggling as well as to those who just need a little assistance. In either case tutors can make a real difference in a student's academic experience. Everyone needs to be held in a comfortable and supportive environment in order to be successful.

The Job Corps

Another interesting possibility is the Job Corps. This program lasts up to two years depending on the entry-level skills of the student. Participants receive academic, vocational, and social training. Successful completion of the program leads to, among other certifications, a GED. The Job Corps has a zero-tolerance policy for substance abuse and violence. It provides a structured, supervised training and residential program, not unlike a military atmosphere, without the ultimate goal of becoming a soldier.

Through linkage agreements between the Job Corps and individual high schools, students completing the program can participate in their home school's graduation, receiving a regular high-school diploma. This is not a quick fix. Students have to qualify both academically and economically, perform to standard in academics and a vocational area, and live with the zero-tolerance policy for drugs and violence. Most students are residential.

Students who are wandering through high school and finding it unsuitable for them can find a home, with the necessary discipline and job training, in the Job Corps. Allowing these students to participate in graduation sweetens the pot. Many students who have completed the program have returned to their home schools as mature, responsible adults. In this way, the Job Corps is not unlike the military, helping students develop self-respect, dignity, and confidence.

The Work Sabbatical

Some students see their jobs as more important than their education. In this case, somehow linking the job to the school program may net results. For instance, one innovative high school developed a program called the Work Sabbatical.

As the name implies, students take a break from school in order to pursue their employment. Remember, however, that a key to working with at-risk students is to maintain contact with them. The work sabbatical does just that. Like any sabbatical, it allows for a temporary leave of absence to accomplish specific goals with the expectation of an eventual return to the regular program. It allows students to remain in school earning graduation credits while they experience the world of work.

Students in the program go to work instead of attending school directly, but they cannot do so for more than two semesters. During this time, their employers have to complete a simple but vital form addressing the performance of the students. Successful completion of this aspect of the program earns credits for one general education course.

The students can expand the program by completing a daily journal about their work experiences. By fulfilling this aspect of the program, students can earn credit for an additional general education course.

Students have to submit their forms and journals to their mentors (teacher or administrator) in the school each week. This ensures that they remain in contact with the school while being gainfully employed. The school accepts the work experience as a legitimate learning activity if it is completed well and up to standards. Meanwhile, the mentor can be planning with the students for their eventual return to school.

See table 2.1 for a sample work sabbatical application form.

Furthermore, the work sabbatical provides a positive connection between the school and the community. The program will not work without community businesspeople who are willing to take the time to become involved with the students and school, completing all necessary paperwork. Some employers may then become regular resources for students in need of this experience, thus becoming an extension of the school's offerings through a mutually beneficial situation.

Part-Time Attendance

While the work sabbatical might be a good idea for some students, others may actually need to work to support themselves or their families. In these cases a partial schedule for several semesters might be in order. This approach needs to take into account whether or not students have to carry a minimum number of credits to be considered enrolled, with possible amendment to this requirement (not unlike the student who attends only a tutoring session).

Some students might remain involved with their schools if they could arrive late each day or leave early in order to maintain gainful employment. If anything, educators should be encouraging those students who are trying to complete an education while having to work as well. If schools can make their lives easier, then why not do so?

Table 2.1 Work Sabbatical Application

Student Name_____
    Date_____
    Description of Employment_____
_____
    Hours/Week_____
    Location_____
    Name of Employer or Supervisor
_____
    Work Phone #_____
    Home Phone #_____
    Why do you wish to participate in this program? Do you plan for one semester or two? What are your plans for school after the program is complete?

Student Signature_____
    Date_____
    Parent Signature_____
    Date_____
    Employer Signature_____
    Date_____
    Mentor Signature_____
    Date_____
    Approved/Disapproved_____
_____
    Reason_____
_____

Table 2.2 Work Sabbatical Weekly Employer Report – Sample

Student_____
Week of_____

Attendance	Acceptable	Not Acceptable
Attitude	Acceptable	Not Acceptable
Work Ethic	Acceptable	Not Acceptable
Punctuality	Acceptable	Not Acceptable
Reliability	Acceptable	Not Acceptable
Completion of Tasks	Acceptable	Not Acceptable
Accuracy of Work	Acceptable	Not Acceptable
Follows Direction	Acceptable	Not Acceptable
Overall Performance	Acceptable	Not Acceptable

General Comments

Employer Signature_____
   Date_____
   Student Signature_____
   Date_____
   Mentor Signature_____
   Date_____

A particular counselor or mentor might be assigned to part-time students, specializing in their particular needs. For these students after hours or early meetings with school officials such as guidance counselors or teachers might be necessary.

Correspondence Courses

Sometimes students fail courses by small margins, such as scoring 55 when a grade of 60 is necessary to pass the course. Obviously, this can be very discouraging. One way to deal with this situation is to use correspondence courses to complete the class failed.

Could students complete credits through correspondence courses? High-school correspondence courses tend to be less rigorous than the face-to-face classes would be. Therefore, it does not make sense to replace the original course with the correspondence course. However, a school might use a formula such as counting the original course 60 percent and the correspondence course 40 percent to create a composite grade.

If this grade were a passing grade, then the transcript would no longer show the failing grade, but the composite grade instead. The student would then earn credit without having to repeat the class.

Let's say that a student failed biology with a grade of 45 percent. He or she could then pursue a correspondence course in high-school biology, and perhaps earn 85 percent. The composite grade would be $(3 \times 45 + 2 \times 85) / 5 = 61$, a passing grade. This approach also supports the idea that some students simply need more time than others in order to learn required concepts and skills to complete a course.

Summer and Standards-Based Curriculum

Another way to approach the problem of failing a course could be by extending the school year for those students who have failed. The teacher would outline what skills and information the student would have to master to complete the course with a passing grade.

Then during the summer, the student would work on these necessary items under the direction of a qualified teacher without having to do the entire course over again. Once the work is completed, the supervisor would give it to the original teacher to evaluate. At that point, if all is well, the course grade could be adjusted and credit awarded.

Many schools have summer programs. Hopefully, this new summer school could be incorporated without too much additional expense. Grants and local business support might be available. If not, then the school has to consider the ultimate cost of a student's dropping out against the advantage of that student's graduation.

This idea of summer school begs the question of whether or not a school is operating with a standards-based program. It would seem that some programs calling themselves standards-based are, in fact, more traditional, seat-time-based systems.

In a traditional system, time is constant but the standard varies. In other words, the school year or semester (the length of a course) is constant. The evaluation, on the other hand, can be a, b, c, d, or f. Thus, there is a range of passing grades, so what exactly is the standard? Can one really say that mastering only 60 percent of the material of a course meets any kind of reasonable standard? Would this be a good standard for a driving test or to become a medical doctor?

In a standards-based system, the standard remains constant, but the time varies. For instance, some students may take more time to reach the standard, and others less time, regardless of what the length of a course is. There would be no grades, just "on standard" or "not on standard." Students would continue to work on the course material until they met the standard, which would indicate that they had mastered, perhaps, at least 85 percent of the material. Only then could they move on to the next level or course.

There would be no failure in such a system. Each student would be moving along at his or her own pace. There would be no credit for 60 percent or even 80 percent, depending on where the standard was set. Using the summer as an extension of the course to allow some students to complete mastery of specific aspects of the course would be an example of standards-based thinking. The idea of year-round schooling appears elsewhere in this book.

Here students could complete a course early or with extra time depending on the situation. In fact, a student should be able to test out of a course, demonstrating mastery of the material on his or her own from other sources of learning. A standards-based system can reduce student frustration and boredom by allowing each individual to progress in his own time and in her own way. This could go a long way in preventing students from giving up on completing a formal education.

Alternative School

Yet another possibility would be to have an alternative school. Some students simply do not do well in regular high school. This can be especially true in large schools where individuals can get lost in the crowd of students. Without connection and the belief that people in the school know and care about them personally, some kids have a tough time engaging in school. School needs to be a safe, caring, and stable part of these kids' lives.

An alternative school is not necessarily about students who are less intelligent or even learning disabled. It is about those students described above, who do not do well in school despite their average or above intelligence. These are the kids who slip through the cracks, have spotty attendance, and eventually give up. They simply do not fit a one-size-fits-all program.

Students would enter the alternative program through an obligatory application procedure to insure that they were sincere and motivated in their desire to be in there. This would happen with the assistance of a counselor or mentor. The program itself would be restricted to a small number of participants to insure a low student-to-teacher ratio. It should also be off campus or in a special area of the school to distinguish it from the program that did not suit these kids' needs in the first place.

The small size of the program would help develop a sense of belonging and community, since teachers and students would get to know each other personally. Kids would work generally independently on those basic skills they are lacking.

An alternative program should include a counselor and a special educator to make it sufficiently self-contained and comfortable, meeting the needs of the participants. The program should be open only to freshmen and sophomores, with the goal of reintegration of these students into the regular program by junior year. The idea, then, is to catch potential dropouts in time to help them be successful and thus remain in school. It is a two-year program, not a complete alternative to the high school.

An alternative program is not a catch-all for students needing something different. There are several possibilities for helping to engage and support at-risk students and those who may be heading toward an at-risk situation, as discussed above. The alternative school is particularly for those kids who are already showing serious attendance issues, or are disaffected, or who simply feel that they do not belong in school. They see school as an irrelevant and uncaring place. The alternative school gives them a place to belong.

If the program is large enough, teachers and a counselor might be made available within the regular staff without the need to hire additional personnel. This further bridges the space between regular and alternative education.

Independent Study

Another idea used to keep students interested and involved in school is the independent study. All too often, however, independent studies are insufficiently structured to insure quality work by the students involved.

It is a rare student who can monitor him- or herself with the self-discipline necessary to carry out a substantive independent study. Consequently, there must be a faculty mentor and a clear outline of what is to be done right from the start.

The beauty of the independent study is that it allows individual students to pursue their specific interests in their own way and at their own pace, thus ensuring continued interest in school. However, as already mentioned, the student will need a plan.

Meeting with a mentor, the student will develop an outline or course of study to define what he or she plans to do. There will be a specific product well defined before the study begins. Together with the mentor, the student can put together a schedule of topics and studies, along with specific dates to meet with the mentor for quality checks and general discussion of problems or other issues the student may be experiencing.

The mentor acts as a guide and expert in the area of the study. Ultimately the mentor will evaluate the student's work and decide if it is sufficient for credit or that there still needs to be more work before the student can consider the project completed.

Ultimate control of the study is in the hands of the student. Hopefully by giving the student control over his or her work, engagement and enthusiasm will increase, and the student will remain invested. An independent study can be seen as a privilege, a reward, and a celebration of individual creativity and learning.

Students who have exhausted the choices that the school has to offer often turn to the independent study as a solution. For instance, the student may have taken the most advanced course in mathematics in the curriculum. He or she must look outside the school for more learning experiences, in this case through personal investigation of higher-level topics. Some students simply learn better on their own. For these students the independent study provides a vehicle to study topics that may already be offered by the school, but in a manner not best suited to their learning styles.

See table 2.3 for an example of an independent study contract or outline.

School–College Partnerships

Partnerships with local colleges and community colleges may be another answer for students who have either exhausted the academic offerings of the school or who simply want to study a topic not part of the school curriculum. Students, if qualified, could take courses at institutions of higher learning, actually for credit. What is doubly effective is having the courses given at the school site. In this case, the college assigns an instructor to the high school, or uses an instructor already teaching at the high school, to teach an advanced course. This can also be accomplished through distance learning.

Table 2.3 Independent Study Contract

Student Name_____
Faculty Advisor_____
Date_____
Area of Credit_____
Specific Topic_____

Breakdown of subtopics for investigation:

Method of study:

Evidence of learning:

Resources needed:

Calendar:

_____
Student

_____
Advisor

_____
Counselor

Successful Completion_____

Unsuccessful Completion_____

Comments:

The community college might be the easiest way to merge high school with postsecondary learning. Because these schools are already in the community, students could even take night courses for dual credit, thus maximizing the benefits of their time at high school. Some students simply need the additional challenge and mature setting of the postsecondary classroom.

Community Partnerships

Building school/college connections or compacts should not be difficult, especially if the school already has a good relationship with the community.

Yet another use of the community could be through internships. The Work Sabbatical was described above. There are also possibilities to work with community members such as lawyers or politicians.

Students could be fully involved, becoming members of committees and at least observing the decision-making process. Students might apprentice with local artists, gardeners, and business people. As with the Work Sabbatical, the school would develop forms to document the student's work in order to award credit for the internship. Some schools have a professional whose job is to work with the community for these purposes.

Testing Out

As mentioned above, if high-school courses are well enough designed with explicit goals and objectives, then testing out of a class becomes another alternative. Some students may already have advanced knowledge in a particular area, such as a foreign language, because the student lived for several years overseas. Other students may have hobbies and interests by which they may have taught themselves sufficiently to test out of a particular course. For instance, a student who lives on a farm may have enough knowledge to test out of a course in basic agriculture.

A FINAL WORD

There are many ways to get an education. A set of traditional courses is only one of them. The central point in attacking the dropout problem is to find ways to keep students engaged in their learning and connected to the school. The more educators can facilitate students' individual ways of learning, the more students will remain in school, or at least connected with school, until their graduation.

One definition of insanity is to do the same thing over and over again, expecting different results each time. The suggestions given here do not include putting students through experiences that have already not worked for them. The school needs the creativity and courage to develop recirculating systems that offer students new routes toward graduation.

It is important to offer supports for those students at risk of falling through the cracks, such as those who are failing particular courses but could do well with just a little assistance. And certainly, if a student has met all of the requirements for graduation earlier than most, there should be the option of early graduation to allow the student to move on to higher levels of learning.

In any case, these ideas involve both minor and significant changes for the institution, board, teachers, and the community. The community can find the resources. More important is the embracing of change. What is suggested here has political and social implications. Do we have the political will to make these changes happen for our children?

ESSENTIALS TO REMEMBER

Schools need to find ways to hold on to students who might be heading for dropping out. It makes no sense to put these students through more of the same, so educators will have to find different methods of teaching and learning to fit these individuals' interests, personal needs, and learning styles. A vital aspect of keeping students in school is to maintain a viable connection between the student and the school.

At the same time these students remain connected to the school, teachers have to offer a kind of freedom to them, allowing them to experiment outside the traditional system.

Some alternatives include the following: all kinds of tutoring, linkage agreements with the Job Corps, opportunities to work in the community such as the above-mentioned work sabbatical and internships, and partial attendance programs.

Students could use correspondence courses to supplement failing grades. Summers would be a great time to extend the school year for students who need more time to complete the given standards of a particular course. For students who have exhausted the school's resources in a particular discipline, there can be independent study.

Alternative schools, in which there is a low student-to-teacher ratio, have the potential to help students feel noticed and cared for. Schools can partner with local institutions of higher learning to create dual-enrollment programs, which would award both graduation credit and college credit.

In all cases, the alternative to the traditional educational process will have to be serious and substantive. The idea is not simply to push students through the system, but rather to allow them to complete a real learning program in innovative and personally tailored ways.

REFERENCE

Zubrzycki, Jaclyn. "New Rules Push Down Grad Rates." *Education Week*, April 4, 2012.

THREE

The Malleable High School: Meeting the Need

WHAT WOULD A BUSINESS DO?

When a business's product no longer appeals to the consumer, something has to happen. The manufacturer may change the product, introduce a new product, or mount a new sales/advertising campaign. The business tries to appeal to the clientele, in this case the consumer. Without some kind of adaptation, the corporation will die. Just think of the phrase "New and Improved."

This is a common situation. Society and its values are constantly changing. Business has to keep up. This is not necessarily a matter of right or wrong, but simply one of continuing relevance and existence. Corporations cannot afford to sit still. Remember the Conestoga Wagon Company? It failed to adapt when wagons were no longer necessary. Does this model apply to the business world only? As in the theory of evolution, doesn't everything have to adapt or die?

The American high school needs to adapt to the needs and changing demographics of its clientele (students) as well. If the goal is to educate all of the American people, then schools must adapt to this widely varying constituency. While there have been many innovations tried and implemented in high schools throughout the country, the basic delivery system and curriculum of the high school have remained fairly stable over the last fifty or more years.

THE BASIC STRUCTURE OF THE AMERICAN HIGH SCHOOL

High schools offer bits of curriculum based on discrete academic disciplines in defined periods of time (forty-five to ninety minutes), usually five days each week, for about 180 days each year. School starts around 7:30 a.m. and ends about 3:00 p.m. There is little or no school during the summer. The school year is divided into two semesters, and the day is divided into four to seven periods or blocks.

Students generally sit in rows, groups of desks, or at times circles. They spend most of their time listening and trying to absorb information. They work quietly at their desks at specific tasks assigned by the instructor. While this may not be the only way to describe high-school classrooms, it is certainly the most common. This is a long-standing structure.

What happens when this one educational format no longer works for a growing part of the population? For instance, some students have jobs during the day, older students who are returning to high school may have both jobs and families, the two-parent nuclear family may no longer be a given, and the job market may be asking for different skill sets than before. To ignore the changing social environment reflects arrogance on the part of schools.

Students with wide variations in experience, values, and backgrounds may be in the same classroom. Educators know that students learn in different ways and at different rates. Is it possible that high school in its current form may be irrelevant for a growing number of potential students?

CHANGES

If high schools are to maximize their effectiveness, then they will have to adapt to changing times. Some of the student population no longer find the time slot between 7:00 a.m. and 3:00 p.m. convenient or even doable at all. As schools become more inclusive, they will have to drop certain assumptions for more accurate ones.

Students learn in many different ways, not only in discrete curriculum bites offered each day. Some students learn more quickly than others; some students need more time. There are hands-on learners as well as those who learn through reading and lecture. The world demands that students learn new skills and knowledge. The high school can no longer insist that students fit themselves to the given structure. The school has to begin to fit itself to the clientele. Otherwise, like the manufacturer, it is likely to become irrelevant.

The New Structure

The ideal school will be open from 7:00 a.m. until 10:00 p.m., all year round. There will be three trimesters of four months each. Students will attend for two trimesters each year, and teachers will work for two trimesters each year. Spreading out the school year will accommodate a more varied student body, but serve those students in smaller groups.

In the best of all possible worlds, there will need to be little change in the number of faculty, since the number of students should be relatively stable. Students will graduate at least three points during the year (at the ends/beginnings of trimesters), and at those same three points new students will be arriving. In other words, there should be an active flow of students into and out of the system.

Such a schedule will have a direct effect on the structure of the school administration. To begin with, depending on the size of the school, there will be at least one principal and two assistant principals. The principal will work year round from 9:00 a.m. to 5:00 p.m. Both assistant principals will work year round, one from 7:00 a.m. to 3:00 p.m., and the other from 2:00 p.m. until 10:00 p.m. Of course, these hours may vary according to daily needs.

This configuration allows for there to be at least one building-level administrator on duty at all times during the extended-day format. There is an overlap in the middle of the day for the three individuals to meet and share information. Complete communication is a key to success in this situation. Each of the three principals will be responsible for one-third of the faculty and students.

However, at any given time one of the three may have to deal with any situation that comes up. All three principals need to know what is going on in the school on any given day. These three administrators form the superstructure of the school governance system.

There will be department heads for each discipline. These professionals, considered administrators, will have a reduced teaching load and be responsible for the administration of their respective departments as well as for the supervision and evaluation of the teachers in their areas. Although department heads will have to work year round, one trimester they will work only half time and not teach at all. (The idea of teachers also teaching only two trimesters is discussed below.) The middle of the day will be reserved for professional meetings.

The department heads will work eight hours each day, but those hours may vary according to daily needs. For instance, on one day the math department head could be working from 8:00 a.m. until 4:00 p.m. to accommodate a meeting and a classroom observation in the morning. On the next day, he or she may be working later into the evening for the same reason.

In a way, the department heads provide the glue for the school's operations, being closer to the day-to-day activity than the principals. Hopefully, the heads will meet as a group frequently, and share information with the principals regularly. Their jobs will be fluid in nature, shifting to fit the needs of the school and their own work on a daily basis.

In this way, the supervision and evaluation of staff and the administration of the departments can continue all year. However, since department heads are also teachers, they too will define their teaching year by two of the three trimesters. Their role bridges the gap between school-wide administration and the daily function of teaching and learning.

These department heads will have to be certified administrators. The function of staff evaluation demands this. Also, they will have to be well versed in their discipline, since they are to be lead teachers, mentors, and curriculum developers. This last function would be ideal as an activity for the nonteaching semester, when the department heads would have more time to devote to these matters. They will also be responsible for budget formation and management. They report directly to the principals.

Other possible administrators could include a director of professional development, dean of students, school/community liaison, athletic director, curriculum director, or supervisor for building and grounds. All of these positions would be year round.

Hopefully, these individuals could take advantage of the time between 2:00 p.m. and 3:00 p.m. to meet with one another to ensure a smooth-running operation. The administrative team needs to be a tight group constantly taking in, sharing, and giving back information so that the school can run as a unified institution. The team links the faculty to the upper administration: the principals and the board of directors.

Teaching and Learning

Teachers would not work all three semesters, but only two. Individuals could opt to have the winter, the summer, or fall semester off as vacation and professional development time. In theory, again, there may not be a need for additional teachers, because running all year means that the regular staff will be attenuated, with fewer teachers working each trimester than would have been working each semester.

In the same way, the student body would be stretched out across the year, with students attending school only two of three trimesters. This is not to say that some students could not attend throughout the year if they so chose. However, this spreading out of the student body would accommodate the idea of having fewer teachers in any given trimester.

Hopefully over time, the school will fall into a rhythm for scheduling. This may take time as the program settles into the new dimensions. There will be more space, both physically and psychologically, as people and programs spread out over a full year. Each trimester will be constructed on the basis of a process by which students preselect courses to determine which will be sufficiently enrolled to run. Classes that are underenrolled may indicate the need to offer independent-study options or other alternative approaches relevant to the subject matter.

The school will be a buzz of activity. The daily offerings to students will include not only independent studies, but also internships, work study, and the like. There will be many ways for individual learners to complete their educations in this new system.

The summer trimester and longer hours would allow nontraditional students to attend classes and work toward graduation in the time available to them. Students could potentially accelerate their programs or make up failed classes by using the third trimester option. Accelerating some students frees time for teachers and tutors to work with those who need a longer period to complete their work.

The optional extra session could also contribute to making school more accessible to various seasonal workers. There would be no problem, for instance, to attending in the fall and winter, or the fall and summer. As long as a student attends for two trimesters each year, then that student will be a typically scheduled student, fully enrolled.

The question of freshman, sophomore, junior, and senior classes becomes moot as students progress at their own rates and come from differing backgrounds. The traditional classification of students by year and age would no longer be necessary or even convenient. The school would offer all core courses during the traditional hours to allow for students who want to complete their high-school education in the standard four years. However, this becomes only one of many options now available for students.

There are real implications for curriculum here. Instead of there being freshman English, for instance, there would be English I. Rather than offer special courses just for adults, the mixture of students in classes removes the stigma for an older student being in a class with younger learners. That student will no longer be alone.

In one classroom, there might be several traditional students as well as students who have returned to high school after being away for years and students accelerating their progress by taking courses all three semesters. Some students have already taken the course but need to take it again to achieve the standards required to progress to the next level. There would be no stigma of age or background, since all classes would be a mixture of ages and experiences.

This situation will allow for a much richer learning environment than the traditional configuration. The variation in experience alone would enrich the learning atmosphere for everyone in the class as they share their various points of view, personal examples, or talents in any given class.

With the traditional four classes no longer necessary, there would also be accommodation for different learning rates and styles. A student gifted in mathematics might complete a course in less than a trimester's time. Some learners might actually test out of a subject. In other words, the new high school would be a standards-based system, where time varied but not the standards. Slower students could retake courses or finish them by continuing after the traditional time of the course was over.

Standards-Based Education

A standards-based system would demand tutorials and small extension classes to accommodate slower or struggling learners. It would also necessitate the writing of a clear curriculum with well-defined standards in each course. This would allow for some students to accelerate their programs by completing standards more quickly than others, or to test out of a course using school-devised tests that address the standards of the course. There would be a consistent measure of student achievement.

Many programs claim that they are standards-based systems, because a number of standards has been defined for each course. However, if grades can still vary from A to F, then what exactly is the standard? If the length of the course remains constant, then how can the system be standards-based? The standards must not vary, but the means of achieving them may.

A great deal of work will need to be done in order to define the standards for each course. Then, there will need to be consistent measures with which to determine if a student has met the standards or not. No student should have to sit through lessons on whatever he or she has already mastered. By the same token, all students need the necessary time for each of them to become proficient in the given standards.

Being a standards-based system is at the core of these proposed changes to the school structure. Therefore, the entire community will have to become involved in the process of conversion from a seat-time to a standards-based perception of how the curriculum works. This simple idea, complex in its implementation, will allow for many of the proposed changes.

The trimester schedule should allow for these variations, particularly acceleration and extended time for those who need these options. The standards-based approach should also allow for life experiences being converted to standards achieved.

Changes for Students

The longer, more open day would accommodate many variations in learning. Internships, independent study, tutoring, half- or partial-day schedules would all be possibilities. In other words, each student could have a distinctive, individual path toward graduation. All students could have their own individual education plans. Many of these options are discussed at greater length in chapter 2 of this book.

The role of teacher mentors for students becomes vital in this system. The flow of education from beginning to graduation is more complex, with more options for progressing than ever before. If every adult in the school were trained to be a student mentor, the ratio of mentors to students could remain low. Thus, each student would gain personal adult attention as well as assistance while planning and implementing his or her educational program.

The mentor's job would be to guide the student through the education process. He or she would help the students select courses, decide on variations such as accelerating in a particular discipline or taking some extra time, or helping to design an independent study. The mentor would also be a sympathetic adult available for the student as a sounding board or an adult adviser.

Mentors would in no way replace counselors, but they would be easily accessible adults who take interest in the individual student. The mentors would have information on each student, such as grades, attendance, special programs, and discipline records to help provide coaching and coaxing. They are a first safety net.

This trimester structure could also have implications for the general student support and discipline system. There would be less stigma in asking a student to leave school until the next trimester begins. This would not have the heavy implications of expulsion. For instance, a student who is a discipline problem or is simply not ready to be a serious learner might need some time away, working or otherwise occupying him- or herself before trying again. The administration could ask the student to leave. The school would always welcome students back, as many times as necessary. Almost all "expulsions" would become short-term, lasting no longer than until the next change of trimester.

Thus, students could move in and out of the system fluidly. Three times during the year, at the beginning of each trimester, students would be allowed to enroll. Students who needed, for whatever reason, to leave school during the middle of a trimester would not have to suffer the problem of a negative transcript. Because this is a standards-based system, the report card or transcript would list only those standards or courses completed at any given time. There would be no failures. There would only be standards met.

Perhaps the greatest advantage would be for those who could not fit the traditional schedule. Former dropouts might be ready to try again, seriously pursuing their educations. Some people might want to improve their skills by taking only specific courses in areas of need. Students who learn better in the morning and those who learn better at night could find courses to fit their biorhythms.

The school thus reconfigures itself to fit the clientele and its needs, no longer demanding that students fit into the one-size education being offered. School becomes more accessible, more relevant, and more viable. It can shape itself around each learner. A student could work all day and attend classes at night. A student could take a semester off if necessary. This fluidity might also allow for a more stable number of students. At any given time, some students might be off while others are on, again balancing the trimesters across the year.

Even though more alternative students would be coming into the school, others will be leaving through three means. The first would be, of course, graduation. Second, students would be on partial schedules and work studies. Third, they could be taking a leave of absence from school. If dropping out became taking a leave of absence, then there would be less sense of finality and failure. The door would always remain open.

Leaving would have less stigma than dropping out does now because there would be a general traffic flow of coming and going. Students could choose to take a few semesters off, try working, or join another program such as the armed forces. Finally, there would, unfortunately, be students asked to leave for the remainder of a trimester for discipline reasons. Once again, this would be a temporary arrangement until the next trimester begins.

Sports and activities would remain virtually the same as ever. Athletics would be subject to the state rules for eligibility by age, as would other activities covered by such regulations. There could be intramural athletics for others. However, organizations such as the art club or French club could be open to students of all ages who were interested.

In fact, any club or organization that does not compete with similar organizations in other schools should be open to all students. Imagine a student council with individuals from fourteen to fifty years of age. Nothing would prevent drama and musical events from happening in the evenings, so they would proceed as they do now. Meeting and rehearsal times could still be between 3:00 p.m. and 5:00 p.m.

THE POSITIVE SIDE FOR CHANGE

These changes will in no way be easy to implement. Old habits and comfort levels die hard, but the changes are to the structure of the high school, not its mission. Teachers will still teach the subjects they have always taught. The delivery system may be different, but here different teachers can find their optimal working conditions, just like the students.

One teacher may be very much into winter sports, so he or she will want to take the winter trimester off. Another teacher may be more of a night person, and thus can elect to teach mainly evening courses. Others will prefer a more traditional day schedule. By giving teachers more options, they will be able to optimize their work situations, and develop better workplace morale.

They will have some control over their work lives. Individual teachers could specialize in independent studies, school–community partnerships, or providing extended learning time for students who need it.

Rather than inconveniencing parents and the community, this school schedule may actually alleviate various pressures. A parent who has to work in the afternoon could see the afternoon as a good time for his or her children to attend school, while there could be more family time in the morning. Employers might be able to offer work hours during the day to students who prefer to go to school at night. The entire school community has more options, more choices, and more room.

All students learn in different ways and have different rhythms to their bodies. They could try to match their optimal learning time to a specific period in the day or evening.

Certainly, there would no longer be complaints of the school lying vacant and useless during a good part of the day and year. While there might be additional expense in maintaining the school all year round, the community would certainly be getting its money's worth out of the building and program.

MAKING THE CHANGE

The central question of this book is relevant once again. Do educators, politicians, families, and communities have the will to live through some difficult changes to make things better? Are all the players ready to work through the tough spots and setbacks in order to produce a new vision of education for all students, not just those considered traditional, who have fit the formula that has remained for so long?

The key to the proposed changes is time. A school system might want to think in terms of a five- or seven-year transition plan. During year one, the system will add several early morning, late afternoon/evening, and summer courses. The staff will begin to rearrange itself to meet the new possibilities. Work will begin in earnest on completing a standards-based curriculum. Gradually, the yearly schedule would change completely.

The school will gradually introduce some new roles. It will develop the new department head system as described above. Teachers and other adults will attend mentor trainings. The three principals will have to parcel out tasks among themselves and develop decision-making and supervisory processes. They will be ultimately responsible for seeing that the school runs as a unified whole.

These three individuals will be responsible for the general running of the school: day-to-day operations, budgets, discipline, curriculum, and teaching and learning. While the department heads will play primary roles in these areas, ultimate responsibility lies with the building-level administrators.

Over time, the school would introduce more options, such as internships, independent schedules, part-time schedules, accelerated classes, and summer course extensions. At the end of the five to seven years, the system should be well on its way to being the ideal described above. There will be many glitches along the way: budgetary, logistical, philosophical, and social; thus the need for gradual but definite change in the direction of the desired outcome.

The steady, deliberate change over time also allows for gradual budget adjustments. New roles, staying open longer, elaborated teaching strategies will have an effect on the budget. Rather than have the entire budget change at once, controlling the rate of change allows for strategic budget planning since the school will anticipate each new shift in the system.

Teachers and administrators will have to do a good deal of homework, researching these ideas and visiting other schools that may provide models for various parts of the new paradigm being sought. After working to reach consensus on the project with the school board, there will have to be a full-out information campaign so that parents and other community member can understand what the school is proposing. Many school community discussions will help lead to clarity, excitement, and the abatement of the fear of the unknown. Everyone must be heard.

Teachers and other educators will need training in their new roles and the workings of the transformed school structures. These sessions could involve philosophical discussions, effects of the changed structures, new teaching strategies useful for the new vision of school, and what opportunities teachers will now have to restructure their own work.

Bite-size pieces. Complete change, all at once, is not likely to work. People need time to adapt to and take in new ideas, especially those that affect their own lives. It will be important to show individuals the parts of the plan that will benefit them, enhancing their experience. In this way, change agents can facilitate buy-in from teachers especially, who will be able to then have a positive image of what is happening.

Who wouldn't mind additional control over their lives, especially at work? What students would object to more options (and therefore control) for the shape and style of their educations? Shouldn't parents be pleased at the newly available options for putting together their day?

Despite these positives, change is still a big negative, involving fear of the unknown, discomfort, and perhaps the loss of traditions and comfortable patterns. If people can be convinced through gradual change, there is a good chance of their being able to weather the storm, eventually seeing that their lives are improved by the new structures and options.

It will be important to illustrate that many of these ideas are not necessarily new. There are already night classes, internships, and standards-based programs. Some schools have mentor systems. Others run summer schools. There are extended-day schedules. The point here is that this chapter proposes a deliberately constructed system that coherently integrates these various pieces into a whole. The envisioned high school constitutes a complete education-delivery system.

The proposed ideas have been tried successfully. But have they ever been attempted in a unified way? This is the change proposed here, that we reinvent schools using the best of what is already out there working. To see that these ideas have been working in various venues should help to encourage everybody involved to embrace these innovations for the benefit of students, staff, and the community.

ESSENTIAL IDEAS TO REMEMBER

If the goal of public education is to provide an education for all Americans, then schools will have to adapt to a changing society and a varied group of students. Essentially, each student brings with himself or herself a set of needs, a set of talents, a unique background, and a place in society.

The basic structure of high school could change to meet these various student and societal needs. The ideal school would be open from 7 a.m. to 10 p.m., all year round. There would be sufficient building-level administrators to be a presence during this entire day. In addition, there would be a strong department head system to provide supervision and evaluation to teachers as well as curriculum development.

By stretching the student population and the teacher population across the entire year, there will be more room for everybody, both physically and psychologically. The open schedule would also allow for many teaching strategies, such as independent study, work study, internships, testing out of a course, extended time to complete a course, and the like.

By no longer having freshmen, sophomores, juniors, and seniors, much of the stigma attached to age and grade would be eliminated. Any given course might have both younger and older students. The school population would comprise a vast array of backgrounds and experiences. Students of various learning styles and rates would be in every classroom.

These innovations beg the question of a standards-based curriculum. To maximize the learning potential of each student, the system will have to move away from seat time. Students will progress through the program at different rates and in different ways. The conversion to a true standards-based system entails tremendous effort and work, but it also provides the necessary coherence within complexity.

Students will have mentors. These will be accessible adults who each mentor a small number of students. The mentors will provide a friendly and safe space for students to talk, and they will advise students throughout their school life in such areas as choosing courses and developing special learning strategies, for example an independent study.

The fluidity of student membership resulting from the trimester system and length of day will have an effect on discipline. Whereas now expulsion is a huge and stigmatizing operation, asking students to leave for the remainder of a trimester will be a less dramatic event. Students will always be entering and exiting the system.

Sports and clubs should see little, if any, change. Teachers will have more control over their work life. They can have a say on which trimester they teach, and develop specialties such as work study programs, independent studies, and extension work for students who need more time to complete a course. They can build a schedule more to their natural rhythms.

Students will also gain more control over their educations. They will be able to choose to attend classes early in the day or in the evening. They will have three trimesters to choose from. Finally, they will have a broad array of options for how they will complete their educations.

These proposals involve enormous change, but the changes have been successfully tried in various schools. The idea here is to take all of these new approaches to education and create one coherent system of teaching and learning.

Undoubtedly, there will be a great deal of resistance to changes of this magnitude. Educators, boards, and community members will have to mount a publicity and information campaign that will give individuals the information they need to understand and embrace this project.

Take the changes slowly. Prepare a five- to seven-year plan to develop and implement the new ideas. Be prepared to write a standards-based curriculum as part of the work. Implement goals one or two at a time. Always prepare the budget with an eye to what is coming next. Communications within the school and between the school and public must remain open and extensive throughout the process.

Certainly what is proposed here is ideal, but not impossible. The question, once again, is whether or not Americans have the political will to make it happen. If we are serious about educating everyone to his or her potential, then we will need an education system that accommodates the many different types of students this implies.

FOUR
Teachers Are Not Professionals

PROFESSION DEFINED

Ask a public schoolteacher if teaching is a profession and if teachers are professionals; the answer will undoubtedly be in the affirmative. However, a close examination of what constitutes a profession casts doubt on this answer. Here "profession" does not apply to paid athletics or to master artisans (commonly referred to as people in the trades). It refers to white collar careers such as medicine, law, architecture, and the like.

Bob Kizlik (2013) includes the following characteristics of professions:

- Professions are maintained as a means of providing essential services to the individual and society.
- Each profession deals with a defined need or function.
- A profession embodies a unique set of skills and knowledge.
- A professional is involved in making decisions about the client.
- Professions are broken up into professional associations, which have a good deal of autonomy with respect to the work of the profession and its surrounding conditions. This may include admission to the profession, professional standards, ethical and performance standards, and professional discipline.
- There is a protracted preparation program for entry into the profession.
- There is a high level of public trust and confidence in members of the profession.
- Accountability for competence is to the profession itself.
- There is little on-the-job supervision of the professional, nor is there such oversight by the public.

In addition, Wikipedia (2013) adds the following characteristics:

Professionals produce high-quality work.

Professionals maintain appropriate relationships with colleagues and clients.

The website "Preserve Articles" adds a code of ethics, truth and loyalty, and transparent work to the list (Preserve Articles 2013). Bill Carroll (1998) reinforces the idea of a professional code of ethics, as do both the American Federation of Teachers (AFT) and the National Education Association (NEA).

One might also consider working conditions and hours. Professionals work until the work is done. They do what they need to do to do a good job, a professional job. They have a fair amount of control over their time on the job and their free time.

One can apply these criteria fairly easily to medicine, law, architecture, psychology, social work, and other professions. However, that education measures up to these characteristics is questionable. This may very well be a result of the way the function and social place of teachers have evolved in this country.

At one time, the teacher was responsible for everything that happened in the school house. This included fetching water and maintaining the wood stove. Teachers were expected to maintain strict social habits, such as not being seen drinking, being with the opposite sex, or being pregnant. Teachers were servants held to a uniquely high moral standard. They taught what they were told to teach. These conditions are not conducive to the defining aspects of a profession offered above.

The situation indicates that teachers are not professionals. Yet society considers them responsible for the education of the nation's children. How can society change this situation? As seen in the other chapters in this volume, there will need to be tremendous political will and trust to make the necessary changes. People will have to share power over the teaching profession, for instance, substituting educator majority boards for the typical school board. Authority for making decisions will have to be ceded from the public to the teachers.

Do sufficient trust and patience exist to elevate teaching to the autonomous level that would allow it to be considered a profession? Will parents be able to loosen their grips on the schools in order to allow teachers and teacher-training institutions to have more control regarding how education in America is delivered? Can people see how the elevation of teaching to a profession correlates with higher-quality schools and teachers?

ESSENTIAL SERVICES TO THE INDIVIDUAL AND SOCIETY

Do public-school teachers provide essential services to society? Certainly providing skills and knowledge, along with social and moral guidelines, to young Americans is essential for our society. Teachers provide role models for their students, and act as referral agents for students in trouble.

Without teachers, all of this would fall to the parents. While parents can and do much of the work, the entire project of educating individual students is an overwhelming task. Only a small number of students are home schooled or sent to independent schools. Consequently, the job falls to the public institutions designed to develop the skills, talents, and attitudes of society's youth. This becomes the role of the public education system, and in that way it does meet this requirement of a profession.

A BODY OF KNOWLEDGE, BEHAVIORS, AND SKILLS

Is there a specific body of knowledge, behaviors, and skills that all public-school teachers must possess? At first glance one might see this as obvious. Of course all teachers need to master common strategies and techniques for such tasks as classroom management and delivery of instruction. However, a quick overview of what each state requires for earning a teaching license reveals that inconsistencies and lack of agreement about that knowledge base abound.

According to the American Federation of Teachers (AFT) Teacher Preparation Taskforce report, "Raising the Bar: Aligning and Elevating Teacher Preparation and the Teaching Profession,"

> We need a systematic approach to preparing teachers for a successful career in the classroom and more rigorous threshold to ensure that every teacher is actually ready to teach. . . . The United States' system is a patchwork lacking consistency (AFT 2012, 1).

The report goes on to say that

> As in medical, law, and other professions, all prospective teachers—whether they come to the profession by the traditional or an alternative route—should meet a universal and rigorous bar that gauges mastery of subject matter knowledge and demonstrates competency in how to teach it (AFT 2012, 1).

Furthermore, the report describes the many stakeholders "responsible for standards, program design, assessment and certification" of teacher preparation programs as a "fragmented tangle" representing groups with "varied, sometimes overlapping responsibilities" (AFT 2012, 8). Clearly, then, education as a profession does not maintain a common, rigorous standard for entry into the profession across all licensing agencies or schools of education.

Medical doctors do meet universal standards, as do lawyers (both individual state oriented and constitutionally oriented examinations). These professionals master a defined body of knowledge and skills.

A Professional Is Involved in Making Decisions About the Client

To some extent this is true for educators. Within their classrooms they have a certain amount of control over how they will approach each student. However, where other professionals work with one client at a time, teachers must work with as many as thirty or more students together in a given time period.

A teacher has no control over whom he or she will see in the classroom. Also, the teacher has to adhere to the school board–prescribed curriculum and methodology, right down to the choice of texts and the rate at which they will be taught. Only within strictly defined limits can a teacher prepare an individualized approach to any given student, unless that student has qualified for special intervention.

Even then, qualification for intervention is highly regulated by federal and state law, not by teacher associations or the individual teacher in the classroom. Once a student is qualified for such intervention, there is an extensive body of regulations defining what this intervention is and how to deliver it, as defined in the Individual Education Plan.

Counselors, therapists, nurses, administrators, special educators, school boards, parents, and state and federal government all have a say in the way the teacher has to serve the client. Of course there are rules and regulations for other professions, but not to the same extent.

For instance, an architect must understand building codes and the nature of various building materials and designs. However, she, along with the client, can decide how to approach the project, meeting the needs and desires of the client through strategies and approaches agreed to between them. The public does not tell the doctor what to prescribe, nor do they tell lawyers what strategies to implement in the courtroom.

Yet in teaching, rules and regulations encumber the professional. Mandated recordkeeping, mandated special units of instruction, mandated social interventions, and the like all get in between the teacher and his best judgment of what might be the most productive way to approach any given student at any given time. Surely teachers make many decisions within their classrooms, but always within this context of complex and numerous demands imposed from the outside.

The AFT report offers the following as one requirement necessary for teachers to be professionals:

> Trustworthy judgment, based on continuous learning in the knowledge base, reflection on experience, continuous inquiry and improvement, and careful consideration of unique contexts and individuals (2012, 14).

Does society at large put this level of trust into its teachers?

One need only think about the No Child Left Behind Act (NCLBA) legislation to see an example of outside pressures controlling teachers' best judgments. All students must, according to the law, meet specific standards at specific times. However, it is clear that all students learn in different ways and at different rates.

Yet, what are teachers to do when their jobs may depend on the students' scores on various evaluation instruments imposed from the outside? The law suggests that all students are the same, which certainly goes counter to what the professional teachers know to be true as a result of their training.

No one tells doctors how much time they have to bring their patients to health. The lawyers unfold their cases as they deem best. Architects can only estimate the time it will take to complete a project. Teachers answer to imposed standards and timelines. In each instance but for educators, the client can object and dismiss the practitioner and look for another. No such connection exists between a teacher and student. They are, more or less, stuck with each other and the curriculum, materials, texts, and methodologies prescribed.

Autonomy—Admission to the Profession

Who controls entry into the profession? Different schools of educations have different graduation requirements, and various states have their own licensing procedures. Some potential teachers have full-year internships, some less. Some come through five-year programs, some take a few extra courses in education while pursuing their bachelor degrees.

One characteristic of a profession is that its members have much to say about who and how individuals enter the field. The AFT report mentioned above says clearly that

> Primary responsibility for setting and enforcing the standards of the profession and ensuring the quality and coherence of teacher preparation programs must reside with members of the profession—practicing professionals in K-12 and higher education (2012, 2).

Most of the preparation programs and licensing requirements are set by bodies that are distant from the actual classroom teacher, such as state legislatures and groups of education professors. Other than through overseeing teacher internships, the vast group of K–12 teachers does not have a say in who enters the profession or how.

One might argue that master teachers supervising interns have the power to prevent a student from becoming a teacher. However, this does not seem to happen often, and the real decision lies with the teacher-preparation institution. In alternative routes to teaching, K–12 educators have even less say. After all, the Education Testing Service writes the Praxis examinations, not professional education associations. Some states have their own tests. Who writes these tests?

There Is a Protracted Preparation Program for Entry into the Profession

Doctors have long residencies; lawyers start as junior partners. Teachers, however, have relatively short internships and are then immediately thrown into the classroom, often with the most challenging students and little support. While some schools have extensive mentoring and induction programs for new teachers, others have very little. Some people estimate the attrition rate for teachers during their first five years is as high as 50 percent. Some refer to teaching as "The Profession That Eats Its Young" (Anhorn 2008). A profession takes care of its members, both during preparation programs and during actual entry into the field.

Elsewhere in this volume, the author discusses teacher induction at length. For now, let it suffice to say that induction programs are inconsistent if they exist at all, and that teaching internships can be very loosely supervised at times. Serious attention needs to be paid to the implementation of thorough and extensive internships and induction programs throughout the profession.

Under the heading entitled "A Profession Governed by Professionals" the AFT describes what an acceptable teacher preparation program would look like:

> A single oversight organization is necessary to establish a widely agreed-upon set of standards, coherent programs and a common set of professionally rigorous assessments to ensure only well-qualified teachers enter the classroom, as is the case in other professions. That organization *should be composed of predominately teachers and teacher educators. Professionals in the field must take primary responsibility for designing coherent standards, identifying what teaching practices are essential for beginning teachers, and designing teacher training so that students are given opportunities to experience and learn these practices. They must also be responsible for ensuring assessments adequately and appropriately identify who is ready to enter the profession* [italics added for emphasis]. (2012, 3)

The state legislature should not be deciding for educators how they prepare for and enter the profession. While certainly there will always be some state oversight and regulation, the primary control in this area should rest with teachers, if they are to be considered professionals.

Autonomy—Professional Discipline and Unions

Each state has some sort of professional ethics board to monitor teacher behavior. Beyond the state level, however, there is little in the way of the teachers monitoring their own. While teaching associations such as the AFT and National Education Association (NEA) may support the idea of teacher ethics, and even have a code of professional ethics, they do little to cull incompetent or unethical members from among their ranks. The AFT report suggests that there needs to be strong peer-to-peer feedback and evaluation within the ranks of the teaching profession to ensure lateral accountability for high-quality professional performance and continuous professional development (2012, 14).

"Educational Association" is a misnomer, especially at the local level. These associations are, in fact, labor unions. Their primary purpose is to protect their members and gain benefits for their members. They do not police themselves. Instead, they negotiate elaborate contracts that shield members from investigation and sanctions.

Tenure brings with it protections of employment for many teachers. While these protections might once have been needed because of autocratic local governments and school boards, these issues are not as egregious as they once were. Now those protections protect the employment of unethical and mediocre teachers. Such protections seem to grow out of a sense of paranoia.

That teachers are organized into unions points to another area in which professional status is questionable. Do professionals have labor unions? Professionals do their work, and they work until the work is done. Teachers, however, negotiate for specific start and stop times and hourly rates of compensation. They negotiate what they will and will not do.

They do not simply take on the challenges presented by teaching and schools. However, to be honest, unreasonable demands are placed on teachers by outside forces. Lawyers and doctors do whatever is necessary to be successful. If a lawyer works more or less, his or her salary varies. Teachers, however, are not compensated for long days, and they are compensated for the times during the school day when they are not engaged in professional activity. What is the source of this odd combination of labor force and professional status?

Who Controls a Teacher's Time?

Again, other professionals can control their time. When teachers are not teaching, they may be required to watch hallways, bathrooms, cafeterias, or study halls, all nonprofessional duties. The community demands that the teaching day must be filled except for brief preparation time. Teachers' time is not their own. They are also required to work beyond contracted hours without pay, for faculty meetings, parent meetings, committee work, or making official phone calls.

By negotiating contracts in the style of labor and management, teachers make themselves appear more like a labor force than a group of professionals. On the one hand, they demand the protections of a labor contract, while on the other they demand to be treated as professionals.

The primary factor in this confused identity is public governance as represented by the school board. Teachers and administrators work for lay boards that hold complete power over curriculum, budget, teaching methodology, evaluation, employment, and the like. There are no qualifications to serve on a school board other than to be elected. One does not need an education or to know anything about teaching and learning or public schools. Can one imagine other professions submitting to this type of governance?

Therefore, with school boards holding ultimate power, teachers need the protection of contracts. Teaching has grown up to be a sophisticated operation, but school boards remain as they were many years ago. This mismatch stands in the way of teachers fully becoming professionals. The situation would be better if there were two strands of governance in educational matters, one for management purposes and one for professional purposes, as one might find in a hospital. The author discusses such a structure elsewhere in this volume.

Until teachers are allowed to govern themselves and not have to bow to politically oriented decision making, they will be workers and not professionals. Individual board members, like many local politicians, often run for office because of a single issue, which they doggedly pursue as a board member. However, the issue may be political and not educational, such as allowing teachers to leave school grounds during the day when they are not otherwise occupied, or setting the hours of operation of the school library.

Because boards are comprised of local individuals, elected by their peers, voters see teachers as public employees who provide a service but also need to be kept in check. After all, the taxpayers are paying teacher salaries, and private-sector citizens can be very hard on public employees, making unreasonable demands. And yet, one does not often see the same kind of oversight for other public servants, such as police or firefighters.

The No Child Left Behind Act and Professionalism

Furthermore, look at what state and federal governments have done to teachers through testing and ranking, at times taking over schools based on their performance as measured by the state. Thus, teachers are politically forced to do what may not be possible or in the best interests of students. That the NCLBA calls for 100 percent of students to be on standard flies in the face of common sense, that students all learn in different ways and at different rates.

This may be the most egregious demand of all. Essentially, the federal government passed into law that all students would be skilled enough to pass a state's evaluation at each grade level. First, reaching 100 percent is virtually impossible, and second, one cannot legislate intelligence.

However, parents and politicians see the promise of the law as a way of getting teachers and schools to do their job. After all, the general public demands these high standards of the schools it owns and funds. And what parent would not want the force of law to guarantee that his or her child would succeed? But would they write a law that required firefighters to be successful each time they battled a blaze?

As long as teachers are subject to this level of governmental control, they cannot be real professionals. The system will not allow them the necessary autonomy to decide what is in the best interests of their clients. This all comes down to a matter of trust. Teachers don't trust that the public will treat them fairly, and the public does not trust teachers to do a good job.

The struggle for control and autonomy creates a vicious cycle, a "catch-22," which keeps teachers from growing into the professionals they claim to be. The more the mistrust, the more teachers have to negotiate contracts. The more they negotiate contracts, the more they look like a labor force and not a profession. Perhaps teacher negotiations should be confined to salary and benefits, allowing teachers themselves to deal with professional issues.

It will take great political will to break this knot. The public should give teachers a chance to police their own ranks and make crucial educational decisions. Of course, this implies that the teacher-preparation programs mentioned above really are rigorous, highly competitive, and teach certain common principles of education. It also demands that teachers be more loyal to their profession than to their colleagues when those colleagues really are not doing an adequate job.

One wonders if this situation is the result of the way teaching and schools were set up hundreds of years ago. Teachers did not have to have many qualifications. They were held to a higher moral standard than others. They were given a clear curriculum and books to teach. They were truly town employees who answered to the public whim. Teachers no longer have to tote water and firewood, but the basic issues of control, trust, and power remain.

HIGH LEVELS OF TRUST AND PUBLIC CONFIDENCE

Does the public trust and have confidence in public-school teachers as responsible professionals? Certainly individuals, until proven otherwise, approach doctors, lawyers, therapists, and other professionals with an assumption that those providers have the necessary skills and knowledge to do a good job. However, this does not appear to be the case with teachers.

Imagine that the NCLBA was about doctors, and that it was called the No Patient Left Behind Act. In this case, the standard for patients to meet would be health. Doctors would be judged on whether or not they could bring all of their patients to good health in a specified time, and according to a legislated definition of what "health" meant.

This standard would apply to all patients despite individual patients' nutrition, income level, type of employment, home life, background, genetics, or disease. Of course, this would be absurd. How different is this, though, from asking that teachers be held responsible for having all students be on standard at the same time and according to the same definition, despite students' varying situations, like those of the doctors' patients?

Why is it necessary for the community to legislate the outcome of teachers' work while not doing the same for other professionals? Apparently, society does not believe that teachers will do their jobs well if they are not held legally liable for doing so, and then they are held to an impossible standard. There will never be 100 percent of all students making the standard, unless the standard is extraordinarily low.

Is it typical for adults to berate doctors and lawyers? They certainly do teachers. Parents frequently defend their children when teachers point out behavior problems and academic issues. Why do they not trust the teacher's word and professional judgment? Why is there so much second-guessing? Society makes tremendous demands of teachers, and then sets up a labyrinth of laws (just think of the Individuals with Disabilities Education Act) to enforce those demands, rather than allowing well-trained teachers to act professionally in their day-to-day work with students.

Society must treat teachers as professionals. However, for this to happen, teachers must act as professionals, starting with rigorous training and extending to taking responsibility for the quality of the members of the profession. A stalemate exists, with both teachers and society afraid to take the first step in dismantling the arcane system of controls and laws and mistrust to allow the necessary changes for education to become a true profession and teachers to be true professionals.

> All our nation's children deserve to be taught by well-prepared professional teachers. For too long, teachers have been treated as technicians, and as implementers of others' ideas. They have been subjected to contradictory accountability demands arising from policymakers and politicians who are often in ideological battle with one another. Consequently, teachers have far too few opportunities to provide input into curricular and pedagogical decisions, and the result is more failed reforms than successful ones. Despite these challenges, upholding teaching as a profession is a task that begins with members of the profession themselves, and it is crucial to improving the learning of K-12 students. (AFT 2012, 14)

Teaching should have professional status. How else can teachers use their professional judgment every day to make the right decisions about the educational programs of their students? Teachers are there, on the ground, with students on a daily basis, so who knows better what those students need? While indeed society, and especially parents, should have a say in the education of the nation's children, it should be equivalent to the input patients have in their doctors' or lawyers' professional decisions.

Teaching will be a profession when teacher training is such that society at large has sufficient trust in teachers' work to free them from overburdening regulations and governance structures.

ESSENTIAL IDEAS TO REMEMBER

Perhaps the best summary of what would constitute a teaching profession is offered by the AFT report cited throughout this chapter.

1. A distinct and essential knowledge base, recognized by both teaching professionals and the public.
2. Trustworthy judgment, based on continuous learning in the knowledge base, reflection on experience, continuous inquiry and improvement, and careful consideration of unique contexts and individuals.
3. Rigorous entry standards into preparation programs and into the profession itself.
4. Preparation programs with a rigorous curriculum and a significant clinical practice component.
5. Participation in developing and sustaining school cultures that can provide systematic, supportive, and rigorous preservice and induction experiences for teacher candidates and novice teachers.
6. Strong, internalized commitments to students and the larger society instantiated in a professional code of ethics.
7. Strong peer-to-peer feedback and evaluation within the ranks of the teaching profession to ensure lateral accountability for high-quality professional performance and continuous professional development. (AFT 2012, 14)

There exists an underlying distrust between the public teaching community and society at large. A major player in this situation is the lay school board, with its complete lack of membership requirements. On the other hand, teachers do not rise to the level of professionalism with regard to policing their own ranks.

Teachers have labor unions, which diminish their professional status.

Teachers are not allowed sufficient control over the profession. They are subject to myriad regulations, rules, and imposed programs. Other professions would not tolerate such density of externally imposed demands. Teachers have little to say about who enters and stays in the profession.

Teachers are not allowed to control their own time. They work extra hours for little or no extra compensation. Yet they are forced to fulfill unprofessional duties such as watching bathrooms and cafeterias as part of their paid performance. They need to be left to complete their work as necessary.

Once teachers have gone through adequately rigorous training to justify their autonomy, then the public has to accord them the respect they deserve, allowing them to make the necessary pedagogical and behavioral decisions with their students. Then, and only then, will teaching be a profession and teachers professionals.

REFERENCES

American Federation of Teachers Teacher Preparation Task Force. (2012). "Raising the Bar: Aligning and Elevating Teacher Preparation and the Teaching Profession." www.aft.org/pdfs/higher.ed/raisingthebar2012.pdf.

Anhorn, Rebecca. (Spring 2008). "The Profession That Eats Its Young." *Delta Gamma Bulletin.* http://dothan.troy.edu/ed/rdavis/PDF%20files/The%20Profession%20that%20Eats%20Its%20Young.pdf.

Carroll, Bill D. (1998). "Engineering as a Profession." http://ranger.uta.edu/˜carroll/cse4317/profession/tsld005.htm.

Kizlik, Bob. (2013). "Characteristics of a Profession." *Adprima.* http://www.adprima.com/profession.htm.

Preserve Articles. (2013). "What Are the Important Characteristics of a Profession?" http://www.preservearticles.com/201201220561/what-are-the-important-characteristics-of-a-profession.html.

Wikipedia (2013). "Professional." http://en.wikipedia.org/wiki/Professional.

FIVE
Logical Leadership: Who's in Charge of School?

SCHOOL BOARDS

The governance of schools is a complex and interconnected process of different types of expertise, skill sets, and leadership positions. The governance of America's schools is problematic from the start. The fact of lay school boards and governmental oversight leaves schools awash in regulations and laws controlled by people who do not necessarily know anything about education or schools.

School boards should work in the realm of policy. However, all too often boards want to become involved with day-to-day operations and minor issues, often at the request of a local constituent. After all, board members are elected locally, which suggests that they should be representing the sentiments of community members.

Because board membership is a political position, individual members may be more interested in getting reelected than in making the hard decisions. If they think politically instead of educationally, then of course it is education that gets short shrift. Often members run for election on a single popular issue, such as reducing the budget or changing the curriculum, without really understanding what these issues entail.

This type of representation may work when there are larger distances between the elected official and his or her constituents, such as those between a state representative and his or her community, or a federal representative and his or her state. The fact that voters have such easy access to their school-board members results in the expectation that community members' individual ideas should be immediately heard and acted upon.

The result, of course, is that schools, administrators, and teachers are not left alone to apply their professional knowledge and skills to the operation of the school as their training would have them do. Rather than working collaboratively, school administrators and boards can find themselves in adversarial positions.

Regardless of the "ought-to-be's," school boards have tremendous power and are not shy about using it. For instance, a board might draft and pass a policy on academic honesty. That would be appropriate. However, when it comes to implementing that policy, the school board should trust the administration and teachers to do their work without extensive and intrusive oversight.

Another way to improve the system would be to require new school-board members to attend workshops in leadership and the function of school boards. Veterans could take refresher courses every few years. In this way, board members would not be completely ignorant of their roles and the function of schools.

When a doctor tells a patient what must be done, the patient may take time to think about the options but then generally trusts the doctor to do what is right. The doctor is the one with the expertise, even though the patient does not have to accept his or her recommendation. However, school administrators and teachers often have to engage in extensive information sharing and persuasion to convince a school board that their ideas are sound and worth pursuing. The subordinate has the expertise but not the authority to act on it. Having a position on the board does not guarantee that one knows what one is doing.

Schools will continue to limp along until there is more trust and collaboration among the various governing and professional bodies involved. Administrators, teachers, and boards should be on the same side, working for the best interests of students, rather than taking adversarial roles. Boards need to trust the school staff to know what is the best thing to do and to be professional.

School members should expect respect from board members. They should not have to beg for the necessary programs and materials to provide a first-rate educational experience. The board sets the broad parameters and the staff makes the direct educational decisions. The boards deal with finance, policy, buildings, bond issues, and the like. School staff deals with students and education.

The hospital board of directors does not tell the doctors how to do their work. Neither should the school board tell school professionals how to do their work. Who is going to tell this to the school boards of America? What school board wants to reduce its power and authority? That school board will have to take a long, hard, honest look at itself and its function, ultimately seeing the bigger picture beyond the political ambitions of its individual members. This will necessitate a major paradigm shift, and a great deal of political will.

THE PRINCIPAL

The job of the school principal is, frankly, impossible. One has to keep the staff, the board, the upper administration, the parents, the students, and the community satisfied. Then there are the state and federal mandates to implement. There is the budget to create and administer. The principal must provide educational leadership and deal with both student and staff discipline. There is the supervision and evaluation of staff. Finally, there are the building and grounds to tend to.

For one person, this is an overwhelming list of tasks. There is more to do than could ever fit into a day, and consequently many principals work very long hours wearing many hats. Is there a way to reduce this burden without losing valuable leadership functions?

One possibility is to look to the hospital for a structure that can apply to the school. Hospitals do not have one person who is in charge of both the professional aspect of the institution and the administrative aspect of the institution. In other words, there are two strands of leadership: administrative and professional.

The executive administrator of the hospital deals with budget, personnel, building and grounds, and the board of directors. There are numerous lesser positions to deal with many of the specifics of running the operation. At the same time there exists another complete hierarchy to maintain the smooth running of the professional (medical) function of the institution.

Within each department there is a governance structure based on longevity of service and depth of skill. The departments have chiefs (of gynecology, of epidemiology, etc.). On a higher level, there may be a medical director and others to oversee more broadly the medical and care function. This leadership line trains and helps evaluate the medical staff. These leaders are less likely to be involved in fundraising or building projects.

Why could not a school have a principal and a chief of staff, one to deal with running the plant and the other the professional function of the institution? This would provide more professional support for teachers and help avoid the conflict between evaluation and supervision inherent in having one person perform both of these tasks. While the principal would be supported by some additional staff, so would the chief of staff be supported by the department heads for each discipline.

The chief of staff and the principal would work as a team and both answer to the board. Teachers would know to whom to go for different types of issues. For instance, a curriculum question would go the chief of staff, while a student discipline matter would go to the principal. The two leaders would develop the budget collaboratively.

This structure might be a little more costly than what is currently in use. However, it would be more professional and hopefully more efficient. The right people with the right skills would be deployed intelligently to maximize the logical and smooth running of the institution.

As it is now, the primary route for advancement is for a teacher to leave the classroom for an administrative position. This makes little sense. Administrators and teachers have overlapping but ultimately different skill sets. Why should a teacher have to leave what he or she does best in order to advance? Would it not make more sense to provide a career ladder that makes use of the teacher's skills, such as master teacher, mentor, lead teacher, department head, chief of staff?

Other teachers with the requisite skills and interest could become more traditional administrators. In fact, school administrators do not have to be great teachers, but they do have to be great at running the plant, keeping order, dealing with personnel issues, and budgeting. Conceivably, one might train to be a school administrator without having been a teacher, again like majoring in hospital or health management/administration without having been a doctor.

American society is too ready to skimp on the professional aspects of teaching. There needs to be a rethinking of the situation and then the political will to make the necessary changes to the internal governance structure of the school and to the function of the school board. These school structures are stuck in the trap of tradition and the need for control.

To break this cycle, some brave community will have to reexamine, in depth, what it is that a principal actually does, as well as what that person is supposed to accomplish, in order to see the fundamental problem. Then once exposed, those weaknesses should be resolved through the construction of a logical system of leadership.

SHARED GOVERNANCE

Another way to share the burden of leadership is through shared governance. This appears to be an ideal possibility, but in reality it is problematic. Philosophical and legal issues can emerge, and personalities have to mesh very well for this option to work effectively.

First, people's motivation must be to work for the good of everyone in the school. Shared governance cannot be a mask for a hostile takeover by the faculty, an attempt to weaken and push aside the administration as a way to grab power. This will only lead to conflict and resentment.

There need to be well-established rules of engagement and division of power. One of the stereotypes for faculty meetings is that they are contentious, and that little if anything gets accomplished. If the body of teachers and administrators are charged with making whole-school decisions then it cannot fall into this trap.

And which decisions does the group make? For instance, they are not going to meet and discuss evacuation when the fire drill is buzzing. On the other hand, they are going to meet and discuss a new student-evaluation system. What about decisions of daily operation, student discipline, or teacher misconduct? In other words, once again there need to be clear definitions of which decisions the administration makes in the course of the day and which require full-group reflection.

The next area for definition is the process of decision making. Does each member get one vote, including the principal? Do the members of the group represent specific groups of teachers, or are they chosen in a general election? Are they appointed? Who does the appointing? How do they communicate with their constituencies? All of this has to be worked out, and then who does the working out?

There is an issue of responsibility that presents problems. Is the principal held responsible by the board for the smooth running of the school? If so, what happens when the principal can see clearly that the group is going in a dangerous direction, but cannot outvote the others? It would be difficult if not impossible for the board to sanction the entire group.

It is easy for a system of majority rule of the group to exist in an ideal world, passing policies and directives for the administration to carry out. But this can lead to unreasonable burdens put on the administration, and then frustration at the principal's failure to carry out what has been mandated. What if the committee decided that all teachers should have a full hour for lunch each day? This would entail contract negotiation, scheduling issues, and potentially issues of student supervision.

There are legal issues as well. Will the group want to deal with teacher evaluation and supervision, teacher misbehavior, and the forms and reports that are designed for the administration to complete? Who is legally responsible for these tasks, and who is licensed to perform them? To whom does the board look for communication, the principal or the full committee?

A great deal of preparation work has to occur before attempting shared governance. Everyone needs to be clear about the purpose of the sharing and in agreement about the decision-making process. There needs to be trust and patience, because there are liable to be any number of missteps along the way.

While collaboration is the ideal form of democratic governance, it is a tricky business. If a school can put together a system that works for all those concerned, then they should go ahead and implement it. If not, then they should think long and hard about the consequences of their actions.

PEER SUPERVISION

An interesting way to relieve some of the leadership pressure and make teachers more professional at the same time is peer supervision. For purposes of this discussion, supervision is a professional growth activity and evaluation is a process for deciding the job status of an individual.

One of the conflicts of the administration is that principals often have to play two conflicting roles: developer and evaluator. It is difficult to work on areas of weakness with the person who is charged with your evaluation. Peer supervision alleviates this conflict of interest by having teachers, peers, provide the supervision for each other.

With the proper training, teachers can learn to be excellent observers of one another and skilled in communicating what they have observed. The process is confidential, the information held between the supervising peer and the supervised peer. The information can be made public only if the observed teacher wants it to be.

The process allows teachers to work together to improve their skills, not just through the observation process, but also through other forms of collaboration such as coteaching, curriculum development, and combining classes for special instructional events. All this experimentation can occur without the fear of being exposed. Without the evaluator, the teachers are freer to innovate and make mistakes as they work toward acquisition of new skills and knowledge. At the same time, the often laborious work of developmental supervision is taken off the list of tasks to be completed by the principal.

The principal would continue to be responsible for teacher performance, and could step in at any point to work individually with a staff member as necessary. The principal could even assign one teacher to work with another who exhibits certain weaknesses. While peers would provide each other with the day-to-day supervision, the principal would continue to have sufficient authority to intervene with a teacher in trouble. An administrator would, of course, regularly (every two or three years) formally evaluate each teacher.

As with all of these reforms, peer supervision can be threatening to the system, appearing to erode the principal's power, or suggest to the board that the teachers are running the school. Trust, information, and political will are all necessary to introduce this process successfully. (For a fuller discussion of peer supervision, see Heller 2004.)

STATE AND FEDERAL GOVERNMENT

Beyond the school board, there are larger centers of control for America's schools that are not necessarily professionally knowledgeable in making decisions about running these institutions. Both federal and state governments legislate mandates for schools that may not always be in the best interests of the schools or the students.

A good example would be the regulations concerning harassment. These include sexual harassment, harassment due to ethnic or racial membership, physical disability, and bullying. It is not unusual to have laws requiring there to be training, complaint processes, and penalties for each of these forms of harassment. This results in a complex bureaucratic system of regulations and systems that might be equally served by a single system for harassment in general. Each specific form of harassment could be defined under the general rule.

The problem is that these types of regulations are political responses to society's ills, not necessarily thoughtful educational responses. After school shootings, there are sure to be many new rules about school safety. When bullying gets national notice, new laws about antibullying appear. Our society does not trust schools to do the right thing or be effective in a number of areas. The results are much time spent in required training programs that are redundant and reporting systems that are duplicative.

The laws assure the public that something is happening while mandating one regulation after another for the schools. Shouldn't schools be sensitive to these issues without having to create arcane and redundant systems for dealing with them? An administration can spend more time dealing with these required projects than with instructional leadership. The schools cannot solve all social problems, as people like to think they should. At some point other elements of society, in particular parents, have to step up.

Perhaps the most odious example of unrealistic controls imposed on America's schools is the No Child Left Behind Act (NCLBA). This law actually legislates student achievement, as if you can mandate intelligence by way of legislation. No educator, or adult for that matter, would deny that all students learn in different ways and at different rates. Yet, NCLBA insists that all students meet specific requirements at the same time. If they do not, the schools are penalized, even to the extent of complete state takeover.

Who, then, is in charge of our schools? The local school board, the state legislature, the federal government, the community? Why do not the professionals operate the school, those individuals trained to do so? Of course there will be some outside regulation, such as safety issues, business laws, and political structures within towns and states. However, the education professionals are best suited to make decisions about teaching and learning, discipline, and curriculum.

Public schools have too many masters. At times, the various agencies creating regulations for schools make contradictory demands, there being little communication among them. There was a time when eligibility for Title I was determined by a test that special educators rejected because it was not fair to all students, and therefore declared unusable. Then there was no vehicle for determining who would get Title I services. The rules for special education are so complex that making mistakes in paperwork and timelines is inevitable.

The bottom line is that society must allow schools to do their jobs. If they fail to do so, then the community should have the right to sanction or reform the institution. A lay community does not have to tell teachers, administrators, and schools how to best educate their students. After all, does the community tell doctors how to diagnose and medicate, or lawyers how to develop their arguments?

Do Americans have the trust to let go? Can they allow schools and trained educators to do their work without interference more than is absolutely necessary? To move to such a system will require not only trust but also political will. Various players will have to give up some authority while others will have to step up to the plate and provide thoughtful, informed, and professional services to students and the community.

In addition, the education profession will have to police its own ranks seriously. There should be no place for poor or even mediocre teachers. In addition, teacher-preparation programs need to develop in their members the necessary skills and knowledge to perform at a level worthy of the public trust.

THE PRINCIPAL AS GENERAL

Society admires strength in its leadership. A leader should be someone who takes decisive action, who jumps into the fray, who is not afraid of confrontation. If the principal does not act this way, people will consider him weak, conflict avoidant, unable to act, or worse, not knowing what to do. But is this always the best way to approach leadership?

Humility is necessary for good leadership. The successful leader does not dominate others or vaunt her own accomplishments. She does not pretend to know every answer or always what to do. As Lao Tzu says in the *Tao Te Ching*, "Do not wish to be shiny like jade/Be dull like rocks" (Lin 2006, 79).

Sometimes, a leader acts too quickly, jumping to conclusions before he knows all the facts. Principals need to know when to deliberately choose to not act. This leaves all options open while he studies the situation, learning about the players, the context, the larger forces at work, and various consequences of different actions, both intended and unintended. The principal keeps all options open until the time for action comes.

People want to be part of the decision-making process, and they do not want to be told what to do. Yet if things do not work out well, then they look to the principal to fix the problem. To do anything less is to shirk one's duty. Of course some decisions are made with decisive action:

there is a fire in the building, there is a shooter in the building, there is a medical emergency. No one will dispute that the principal must act immediately and decisively or risk more than his reputation.

As Lao Tzu writes, "The people's difficulty in being governed/Is due to the meddling of the ruler" (Lin 2006, 151). This admonition against micromanagement can be applied to all levels of leadership: government, board, principal.

Some problems, if left alone, will solve themselves. Two teachers are unhappy sharing a room because they cannot work out a way to share the bulletin board space. They come to the principal for a resolution. Rather than making a decision, the principal can simply leave it to the two teachers to work things out. In this way, the principal does not have to alienate one or both parties by making a decision that will inevitably be unacceptable to someone. Only if the two teachers cannot come to terms with their problem should the principal act.

Trying to impose one's view or method on the world rarely works. Principals who try to control the environment often run into resistance and are perceived as autocratic. In any situation, there are various natural forces or tides that one can fight, but generally not overcome. A teacher reads the newspaper during every faculty meeting. The principal has asked him to stop repeatedly, but to no avail. The principal could be heavy handed and formally reprimand the teacher, but this will result in lasting ill will. Perhaps she should try to understand why the teacher behaves in this way, and then work to correct the source of the problem.

Rather than trying to control a situation, a good leader will work with the natural momentum of a situation. Many students cut study halls. They think that study halls are a waste of time. Their parents support them in this idea, although they do not support skipping class. Trying to control this issue by punishing students for not going to study halls will open endless conflict and probably a lack of parental support. Lao Tzu would suggest that one "Act without action/Manage without meddling" (Lin 2006, 127).

A better solution might be to find something for students who do not want to go to study hall to do. This is a positive step, supportive of students' desire to do something worthwhile. The principal does not take the general action of trying to control what is going on. He does not meddle with the needs and desires of the students. As a bonus, parents will be happy that their children are engaged in productive activity. The principal works with the natural flow of the situation. By "losing" the battle (not being able to force students to attend), the principal has actually won.

AN EXAMPLE OF CONSTRUCTIVIST LEADERSHIP

In *The Constructivist Leader* (2002, 106–7), Lambert et al. offer strategies for avoiding meetings in which each participant argues a position, thereby effectively shutting down anything like discussion. Imagine a faculty meeting to decide whether or not students should be allowed to wear their hats in school. The effective leader will help teachers to see the complexity of the situation, not just allow them to vent their frustrations.

Immediately, individuals stake out their positions. They proceed to state their finished opinions at one another. The result is immediate stalemate. However, a successful leader will pose the issue differently. She might ask for teachers to think about the reasons students have to wear their hats. This question would be followed by a pause, during which people think about the question the principal has posed.

Then the principal elicits responses. The comments now are not why kids should or should not wear hats. They are more thoughtful, trying to understand the students' point of view and to contextualize the situation. All thoughts are written on a flip chart or the board. When everyone who wants to has participated, then the principal asks that each member of the group write down what he or she thinks about the issue. This question is not a should-or-should-not question. It is more complex than that and demands reflection.

Finally the principal collects the responses. The meeting ends, but before the next one, the principal will have collated and summarized the responses as the basis for a discussion of what to do about the situation, if there is anything to do at all. The good leader avoids dead-end discussion topics, and instead poses questions that demand thought and reflection. This is the principal taking action without offending or alienating anyone. This is the principal "not acting" at all, but simply allowing the conversation to take place. The results are rich and useful, promoting conversation rather than stifling it.

THE ROLE OF PARENTS

Parents play a complex role in school governance. They send their most precious possessions, their children, to school and give their care and nurturance over to people who may actually be strangers. The school asks for their trust sight unseen. Parents are their children's first and best teachers. All of a sudden society asks them to share that role. Consequently, there is no surprise that parents are so concerned about and involved with the public schools.

In one way, parents can exert tremendous political control over schools. They elect the school board. If they do not like the way a particular board member is influencing a school, then they can vote that member out of office. On the other hand, parents can organize to elect a majority of board members who hold views and philosophies with which they agree. Once again, politics can determine the direction of a school as opposed to expert opinion on what is best for the education of the students.

Parents can participate directly in the governance process by attending board meetings to make their views known and by serving on board committees at times. They have easy access to their elected representatives. Superintendents and principals hear directly from parents through phone calls, notes, and meetings. A parent could bring complaints as specific as requesting that their child get more playing hours on the varsity team. Of course, they can also bring good news, compliments, and encouragement.

Parents who are politically influential, the leaders of the community, may get more access and response than other parents. Groups of parents can exert great pressure on board members or school officials. Sometimes they befriend specific teachers and then press for the interests of those teachers. This can empower teachers to skip over the administration with their issues and go directly to parents or board members, thus disempowering the principal and the governance structure in general.

Unfortunately, parents often fail to see the big picture as they advocate for actions and policies that are generated from their concerns for their individual children. For instance, a parent or board member might expend great energy arguing for an open campus so that his child can go to work earlier in the day. Obviously, there is a bigger picture here, one that affects all students, parents, and the community in general. Failure to see the big picture results in personal requests that may or may not be relevant to the discussion of running the school.

Schools need the support of parents. When parents always take their children's side in disciplinary or curricular issues, the school's ability to fulfill its mission is limited. The problem, as seen throughout this book, is one of trust. If the parents trusted the school to do its job, then they would interfere less, thus allowing the school to act in the best interests of all students. Parents will have to accept the professional opinion of the school as some point, relying on the training, experience, and professionalism of the staff.

Can this be done? Can parents allow their children to experience negative consequences of behavior infractions or poor academic performance, rather than helping them avoid responsibility for their own errors? Without doubt, it is very difficult to watch one's own child have to deal with these kinds of difficulties. However, is not one of the functions of schools to inculcate community values, thus necessitating holding students to specific standards? How else will the kids learn to become independent, respectful, thoughtful human beings?

Clearly, the change being suggested here is simple but difficult. Asking parents to give up their children to another authority, even for a few hours a day, clearly flies in the face of their wanting to protect and nurture those children. This will take a leap of faith, an act of will and trust. When parents can give over to schools some of the responsibility for their children, then the schools will be free to work with individual students in ways their professional training leads them to see as productive.

ESSENTIAL IDEAS TO REMEMBER

School boards wield tremendous power over schools, yet there are no requirements to serve on the board. Therefore, often individuals who know very little about running institutions in general and schools specifically get elected. Because their positions are political and the electorate is very close to these officials, they feel they have to respond to every suggestion or complaint they receive.

This leads to micromanagement by board members, when they should be dealing on the level of policy and allowing teachers and administrators to use their professional judgment. Once again, a major issue is trust. Perhaps if school-board members had some required training in their roles, schools might run more smoothly and professionally.

The principal's job is an impossible one. There is simply too much to do and keep track of. On top of that, there can be a conflict of interest if the principal both evaluates teachers and is also responsible for their professional growth activities. One solution may be to look at the hospital model, where there is a hospital administrator responsible for running the organization and a chief of staff responsible for professional matters. The two could work together, but no longer would these two jobs be combined into one overwhelming position.

Shared governance can alleviate some of the burden of leadership from the principal. However, it is fraught with its own complexities that can create a situation that may be worse than having all authority rest with the principal. Schools should enter into such governance structures with careful thought and extreme caution.

A way of taking some of the pressure off the principal and making teachers more professionally responsible is to use peer supervision. In this model, teachers are trained to work with each other as peer observers and coaches for professional development outside the realm of evaluation. This would eliminate any conflict of interest, and at the same time do nothing to diminish the authority of the principal.

The state and federal governments impose a great many burdens on the school system. Once again the matter of trust arises, since so many of these laws (i.e., Individuals with Disabilities Education Act and NCLBA) make what are at times impossible demands of schools rather than trust them to do the right thing with students in need.

People need to stop seeing the principal as the general who makes rapid decisions and jumps into every fray in the name of active leadership. Much can be accomplished through waiting, collecting information, and then acting with deliberate strategies designed for the specific situation.

The educational leader can use the principles of constructivism to involve people strategically and productively in school governance.

Parents will have to learn to trust the professionals in their children's schools. Through board elections and meetings, they can exert their own brand of micromanagement rather than allow the paid professionals to do their jobs. This will take a leap of faith, but it will result in a more organized and smoothly running educational system.

As seen in other chapters, these changes will require political will. Teachers, administrators, board members, government, students, community, and parents will all have to take a risk, learning to trust the schools to do what is right. Once all of these constituents can take this leap of faith, then the schools will be on the way to creating logical governance systems which rely on the training and professionalism of the individuals who work in those schools.

REFERENCES

Heller, D. (2004). *Teachers Wanted: Attracting and Retaining Good Teachers.* Alexandria, VA: Association for Supervision and Curriculum Development.

Lambert, L., D. Walker, D. Zimmerman, J. Cooper, M. Lambert, M. Gardner, and M. Szabo. (2002). *The Constructivist Leader*, 2nd ed. New York: Teacher College Press.

Lin, Derek, trans. (2006). *Tao Te Ching Annotated and Explained.* Woodstock, VT: Skylight Paths Publishing.

SIX

We Owe It to the Profession: Nurturing the Next Generation

PROFESSIONALISM

As a rule, the teaching profession is not good to its newest members. Teaching has one of the highest attrition rates of all professions. First-year teachers are often left to figure things out on their own, asked to teach the most challenging classes, and made to staff the least-preferable duties. Seniority too often rules in these cases. However, in reality shouldn't the best teachers teach the most challenging courses? Shouldn't someone take care of the new teachers by supporting and guiding them? By giving them the time they need to acclimate and learn the system?

Once again, the suggestions that follow may already exist in some places, but they are not yet the rule. Most of what follows is not costly. Some districts do fund such programs through district professional development budgets and federal grants. Many districts will pay for some teacher course work, and this money may also be available.

However, the suggested programs and attitudes below may fly in the face of tradition. Experienced teachers expect to reap the benefits of seniority. So, the question becomes: do teachers have the will to change, to share power, to take on what may be difficult for the benefit of the new teachers, the students, and the profession? The changes themselves may be relatively easy, but being willing to make them is the challenge. Professionals can and should help select and take care of the newest members of their profession.

The profession will also have to convince school boards that a major function that schools as professional organizations have to perform is the development and nurturing of new generations of teachers. This idea necessarily diverts resources to new-teacher preparation and induction, away from the other operations of the school.

Teachers and administrators need to demonstrate to boards the high attrition rates of new teachers and the expense of hiring, both in terms of time and money, but also in terms of lost experience and potential. Professional development does not only occur outside the school walls, but within them as well. Boards need to see that programs for aspiring and new teachers are not just an expense, but also an investment.

Boards cannot simply expect that all great teachers become so as the result of trial by fire. New teachers will need guidance and a helping hand to hone their skills and learn the system. Just think about all of the inservice programs experienced teachers already have, while the new teacher has had none of those trainings, but is expected to perform at the same level as others.

Can boards and teachers see beyond today and make the sacrifices and investments that will result in a more effective teaching and learning community? Change is never easy, but schools and the teaching profession cannot grow and improve without it. Too often such growth takes a backseat to other budget concerns, when in fact it may result not only in better teachers but also in actual fiscal savings in the long run.

Teacher involvement in the development of new teachers is vital in two ways. First, one mark of a profession is gatekeeping. Teachers should have a significant say in the nurturing and qualification of the next generation in the field.

> Individuals in a field occupy one of three major roles. The elite are *gatekeepers* who preside over the destiny of the professional realm and judge which changes in domain should be sanctioned. Some fields recognize a hierarchy of gatekeepers, whereas others do not. Gatekeepers emerge as a result of complex interactions among practitioners that involve politics, reputation, respect, and appointment to key institutional positions. In medicine the ranks of gatekeepers include the medical directors of major funding institutions such as the National Institutes of Health (NIH), the deans and department heads of major medical schools, the editors of respected medical journals such as *The New England Journal of Medicine*, and *The Lancet*, and so on. (Gardner et al. 2001, 25)

Second, the profession owes prospective teachers adequate and supportive training opportunities to ensure they have a positive and substantive experience as they decide to become educators. Schools do not want to lose good new teachers, and experienced staff do not want to lose promising colleagues.

KNOWING WHAT ONE IS GETTING INTO

Many prospective teachers first experience the classroom through internships when they are college seniors or in MEd programs. How sad to find out at the end of one's education that teaching is not a suitable profession. Why do we make students wait until it is too late to change to find out if teaching is the field for them?

Students who think they might like to become teachers should have the opportunity to experience life in a public school early on in their education, before they have invested a full four years in postsecondary institutions. This would be like asking a potential instrumentalist to perform with a world-class symphony orchestra before ever having played even a duet.

For instance, prospective teachers, as college freshmen, could spend a couple of hours each week in a local public school observing and perhaps doing a bit of tutoring. This would begin to get the student acclimated to schools in general, and to begin to develop a sense of what a teacher's work environment is like.

During sophomore year, the student would continue to observe and spend a specific number of hours in structured tutoring of students. During junior year, the budding teachers could actually intern for a month, which would include some coteaching, some solo teaching, attending faculty meetings, and perhaps working a bit with parents.

The senior year would be time for the full internship, during which a prospective teacher would experience all of the aspects of the profession: planning and teaching lessons, dealing with discipline, attending parent conferences, attending faculty meetings, working in teaching teams, and awarding grades.

By following such a schedule of gradually increasing immersion into the profession, students would be able to determine whether or not they truly wanted to become teachers before they were literally about to graduate from college, when changing career paths can be quite difficult.

The result would be a set of first-year teachers who are ready and eager to take on the challenges of the job. Hopefully, this would result in fewer individuals leaving the profession in the first few years of their employment, after having found out that teaching was not what they had expected it to be. Morale, involvement, and expertise would all benefit from this gradual introduction to working in schools.

THE TEACHING INTERNSHIP

The teaching internship is the time for the preservice teacher to test her skills, refine technique, learn new strategies, and work with actual students in actual classrooms all before setting out to search for that first professional position. This is the crucial aspect of teacher training, yet there is little consistency in internships from one institution to another.

Some alternative preparation programs offer short internships, others extensive ones. Minimum characteristics of the internship program should require the following:

1. A teaching internship of at least one full semester, preferably two, offering as full an experience as possible. The internship should include not only teaching but also the various other tasks of a teacher in a public school, such as parent conferences and faculty meetings.
2. Training for cooperating teachers in techniques for supervision and communication. Being able to carefully observe and give useful feedback to aspiring teachers is not an inborn skill. It requires training and practice. There is trust building to be done here as well.
3. Extensive field supervision, merging the school and the sending university, allowing supervisors to work in tandem. The university should not abandon the student to the school, but rather be a strong presence giving guidance and direction to the student.
4. A support group for interns, giving them a safe place to vent. Student teaching can be lonely. Knowing that others are sharing your experiences, both positive and negative, can be comforting. Interns can exchange strategies for dealing with various issues.
5. A support group for cooperating teachers, so they do not feel alone. These teachers also need to share both positive and negative experiences and strategies for dealing with their interns.

The Full Experience

Interns should be totally immersed in the life of the professional.

> Interns need to be encouraged, if not required, to participate in all aspects of the school as any teacher would. They should sit with their cooperating teachers during parent conferences. They should participate in supervisory duties. Interns can be members of committees, and they can help coach athletics or advise clubs. (Heller 2004, 25)

All too often, interns are left to fend for themselves. They can be dropped in a classroom and then given little support or instruction after that. The college or university should be providing active supervision and instruction. Frequent observations and the time to reflect on them with college personnel are vital. The university is like the parent of a child trying to ride a bicycle without training wheels for the first time. The field supervisor and the cooperating teacher should be meeting regularly to discuss the progress of the intern.

A player who often gets forgotten is the cooperating teacher. Through generosity or professionalism or both, the cooperating teacher opens his or her classroom to the intern and provides structure and wisdom to the practice period. However, the skills to be a cooperating teacher may not be innate.

The teacher will need training in supervision techniques and communications. He will need a set of standards or competencies, such as those described by Charlotte Danielson in her book *Enhancing Professional Practice: A Framework for Teaching* (1996). The college may already have a set of teaching competencies that they use to inform their evaluation of the intern.

How will the cooperating teacher become familiar with these competencies, understand them, recognize them in practice, and know how to teach them? This will necessitate training. Hopefully, this learning experience will lead to some credit awarded to the teacher. There is enough material for a full graduate course here.

Additionally, being a cooperating teacher can be lonely. A public school with a truly professional atmosphere will want to establish a reflection group of all the cooperating teachers at any given time. These teachers could meet once a week to reflect on what is happening with their interns and share strategies. Someone from guidance or the administration could facilitate the group. Cooperating teachers should not be left to perform on their own without support.

Finally, the interns will need a support group of their own. A member of the college or the school staff could facilitate this weekly meeting. Here interns would reflect on their experiences, perhaps keeping journals, and sharing problems they are having as well as possible solutions for them. It is a good idea to have the interns keep journals, thus providing questions, solutions, and topics for conversation. What interns say in this context will be held confidential, thus allowing them to speak freely. A facilitator who is not directly involved with the internship process might be best.

The internship process should be both nurturing and clearly evaluative. In other words, it is not a formality in becoming a teacher. It is a capstone learning experience. Some interns will not perform adequately and therefore not become licensed. The college and the school should have methods for combining their information about the intern and making a shared decision regarding credit for the experience. Again, a set of teaching competencies and strategies, and the standards interns must meet, should be clear and understood by all parties.

HIRING NEW TEACHERS

As mentioned above, deciding who does and does not enter the profession is called gatekeeping. Teachers and schools play a key role in this process. While institutions of higher learning and professional organizations certainly have gatekeeping functions, it is at the level of the individual school that the decisions of hiring new teachers occur. Additionally, most new teachers serve a probationary period before becoming regular members of the staff. Schools have the right to dismiss the teacher during this period if he or she is not performing adequately.

A school's philosophy can be a crucial factor in successful hiring. The clearer statements of philosophy, mission, and vision are, the more precisely schools can hone their searches for new teachers. In fact, the philosophy could become the basis for establishing job descriptions and interview questions. By hiring personnel on the basis of their compatibility with the school's philosophical beliefs, the school sets a direction for its own development and a consistency for its daily operation.

> A consideration here is the philosophy of your school. How can you know who will fit well with your institution if you do not know who you are? What does your school stand for? What is its collective attitude toward children, teaching, learning, professional development, and discipline? To match new hires to your school, you need to know what you are matching, and that means you need a clear statement of institutional identity. (Heller 2004, 41)

One caveat: the philosophy must actually be the result of many discussions that include the voices of board members, administrators, teachers, paraprofessionals, other support staff, students, parents, and other community members. In other words, there has to be buy-in for the philosophy, and everyone's understanding that all decisions or actions taken are made based on that philosophy. A more complete discussion of the creation of a philosophy and its use in hiring teaching personnel can be found in Heller 2004.

> The principal is going to be held accountable for the success or failure of those he or she hires. Therefore, after the major ideas of the philosophy emerge from . . . larger community conversations, it is the principal's job to convert that language into useable terms. (Heller 2004, 47)

Those terms become the basis of the interview questions.

For instance, if the school places a premium on teachers' liking kids, then some of the following questions might be useful:

1. How is your teaching student centered? Could you describe an example of how you empower your students?
2. How do you show respect for students? Relate some incidents where you clearly showed respect for students.

3. Can you give us an example of how you have fun with your students? What are some activities you have used that are both educational and fun?

Developing interview questions based on the school's philosophy makes sense on two levels. First, it would not be fair to the new teacher if she were put into a situation that ran counter to her beliefs. How could the new teacher survive in an incompatible atmosphere? The teacher and school want a good fit. Thus, using the philosophy has another advantage, which is to forward the particular school's mission and beliefs by hiring individuals who embody them.

> If new teachers find that the school complements their own style and beliefs, then those teachers are likely to be comfortable and productive, and they have a good chance of having their professional needs satisfied by the school's climate, practices, and beliefs. Obviously, such teachers will be more apt to remain in the profession and in that particular school than those who do not fit in with the school's value system and feel out of place, disillusioned, or frustrated. (Heller 2004, 41)

Any good interview process will include a committee of teachers as well as the principal. After all, the new hire will be working closely with these teachers, and who could be better at determining compatibility? The process also honors teachers as professionals, allowing them some significant gatekeeping authority.

NEW TEACHER INDUCTION: MENTORS

How do schools take care of their new teachers? Is there an adequate induction process in place to help them to a successful beginning in this complex and often frustrating profession? No matter how thorough their preparation, new teachers are not fully prepared for the day-to-day operation of a school and their own classroom. Practicing is not the same as being in the real game.

New teachers need mentoring. This does not mean simply assigning the new hire a buddy. A mentor needs to be a highly qualified guide, coach, and confidant. Being an experienced and well-liked teacher does not necessarily make one a good mentor. A mentor needs training and support in order to do a quality job of guiding the new teacher through a successful first year. It is not fair to the teacher or the mentor to use mentors who do not have any knowledge or expertise in the mentor role. The mentor is the teacher's main lifeline during that first critical year.

A good mentoring system will involve the local college or university if at all possible. The institution of higher learning can provide the necessary training and support for the mentor, who must have supervision, counseling, communication, and personal relations skills. Ideally, the mentor should be teaching in the same area as the mentee. In addition, the mentor will need time and compensation.

If the mentor does his or her job well, compensation will be far less expensive than the cost in time and money of hiring new teachers for the same positions every few years. A lightened teaching load, as opposed to a stipend, might be adequate payment for the mentor's service.

To insure quality mentors, there should be a written application process. The application will go before a teacher review board, and it will be anonymous. Once the board approves of an application, then its members can interview the candidate. This process should help alleviate the possibility of the mentor's position being just another "good old boy" perk. This is serious business. Being a mentor is not an entitlement, but an earned position.

The district will develop a pool of mentors that it can call upon as necessary. Becoming a mentor is open to every teacher. However, applying does not guarantee success. In fact, a teacher may go through the process only to find that he is not considered qualified or that there are no available and appropriate mentees at a given time.

As mentioned above, the mentor will undergo formal training in the skills of mentoring. She will need to be willing to devote time and caring to the new teacher, to meet on a regularly scheduled basis and as needed. The mentor is a friend, but also a means of professional development for the mentee.

The school and mentor should see mentoring as a professional activity, part of the gatekeeping process. As with cooperating teachers and student interns, it would be wise to have the mentors meet as a group periodically as well as have the new teachers meet as a regularly scheduled group. Especially new, but in fact all mentors, need a place to solve problems and share ideas.

Such peer groups give new teachers and mentors places to get support and encouragement. Furthermore, individuals can bring issues to the group for discussion of possible causes and solutions to various challenges. The group, hopefully, provides a safe place for professionals to speak their minds without fear of what they say being repeated beyond the session. Someone from the university could facilitate the new-teacher group, and the mentor group could choose one of its members to run their group.

Finally, there needs to be a means for the groups' ideas reaching the people who are charged with considering issues or problems in the system's new-teacher induction. This could be accomplished by having the minutes of each session, reported without names or identifying characteristics, to such individuals as building and central administration and personnel from the university.

THE NEW-TEACHER COURSE

Recent graduates of schools of education may know a great deal about teaching strategies, but they may not be ready for the "boots on the ground" work of a teacher. For this, they will need some inservice training to run parallel to their first year as professionals.

One excellent way to accomplish this training is with a new-teacher course, taught by an experienced member of the district. The course can deal with topics such as:

1. Engaging in a successful parent/teacher conference. What skills are needed here? How can one avoid conflict, or how can one resolve conflict? Who is the meeting for, and who is in charge? What is the purpose of the meeting? When does a teacher need to ask for help? Ultimately, who has what authority?
2. Methods of classroom control and student discipline. What strategies does the teacher already know and can share with others? What is discipline with dignity? What is student-centered discipline? Can discipline issues be avoided? How? The teacher leading the group could have the district behaviorist as well as other experienced teachers in to offer strategies of classroom control and the development of positive student–teacher relationships to the new hires. How does district philosophy inform student discipline?
3. The local special-education process. How do you make a referral, to whom? What steps does a teacher have to take to work with a student before the special education process kicks in? Does the district use Response to Intervention as a support tool for students? Who can help in this area? What are the teacher resources? Is there someone in each building for the teacher to turn to for assistance?
4. District and school curriculum. Is there a set curriculum for your area of instruction? Who monitors this? What does the curriculum coordinator do? How does the principal or department head fit in? What are the teacher's obligations with respect to the curriculum? Where can one find the necessary curriculum documents? What is the process for amending the curriculum? How much can the teacher be inventive and original in delivering the curriculum? What is the process for selecting books and materials?
5. Guidance and other student support systems. Who are the guidance counselors and what services do they provide? Will they help facilitate parent/teacher meetings? Will they work with the teacher together with a problem student? Do they serve as liaisons between the school and community opportunities? Can a teacher seek out a guidance counselor to discuss problems related to the job, and will these discussions be truly confidential? Are there oth-

er support personnel such as a school psychologist, a school therapist, or special programs for challenged students?

Individual class sessions will host guests, such as the director of pupil support services, the special education director, or perhaps the curriculum director. These classes and personnel will enable the new teachers to integrate into the profession generally and the district specifically. Becoming familiar with key personnel in this setting helps to break down fears. Teachers and specialists can speak openly together in the class sessions, which will hopefully spill over into actual job situations.

If a local college or university can sanction the course and award credits for it, then the new teachers will be on their way toward professional development and advancing on the pay scale as well. Teaching this course, mentoring, and being a cooperating teacher should also bear college credit, salary advancement, or relicensure credits. Furthermore, this will help strengthen the relationship between the district and the institution of higher learning.

The course is best taught by someone in the district. There is credibility here that cannot be duplicated by using someone from outside. This class is about working in this particular place as well as about the profession generally. Therefore, someone who knows the particular system best is well suited for the job. This arrangement also underscores the caring for the new hires as part of the profession, and shows the person teaching the class as a responsible member of the profession—university, course instructor, mentors all working together to help ensure a successful first year.

COMMUNITY INDUCTION

The school community is likely not the only one that will be new to the first-year teacher. The actual social community, the people and the town, may be unknown as well. A dinner or luncheon for the new teachers and mentors can help with this.

First, district members could explain the general structure of the school system, who does what, where to get various types of assistance, along with phone numbers and offices. Then, with the help of mentors, experienced personnel can introduce the neophytes to each other, the town, and its resources.

A member of the Chamber of Commerce might describe where someone can find specific resources, such as hairdressing, groceries, gasoline, housing, and the like. A member of the select board or mayor's office could speak about libraries, town events and meetings, or where and when to register to vote. Each new teacher should leave this session with a map of the town and of the district. Perhaps the event could serve as the first class of the new-teachers' course.

This is a time for mentors and mentees to sit with one another in a social setting, away from the rush of school in session. Time for friendship and bonding to develop can be very effective in making the new teacher feel comfortable in his or her new surroundings.

WHAT IS THERE TO DO?

The right thing to do, as a profession, is obvious. Educators have to become more serious and comprehensive about training and supporting new teachers, both preservice and inservice. The necessary tasks, as described above, can be complex and time consuming, but they are in no way impossible or wildly idealistic. The necessary requirement for their implementation is political will.

Change is inevitably disruptive, demanding that people perform in new ways that interfere with their comfort zones. There are teachers who will not want this additional professional responsibility. There are school systems that will not want to disrupt their established way of business to accommodate this new way of looking at teacher training. Schools and universities do not always get along easily.

School boards will have to agree that teacher training and induction is sufficiently important to invest the necessary time and financial support to make these new programs flourish. Teachers must convince politicians and the public of the benefit of spending more time with pre- and inservice teachers.

The crucial point is to show how tending more carefully to teacher training and induction will result in benefits, both in the education of the students and in financial advantages. There is little to suggest that all of this additional and directed training could result in anything but better teachers, even if it simply convinces more people who think they want to be teachers to reconsider their career choices.

Financial benefits may be more difficult to demonstrate. Certainly regular teacher turnover is costly. Hiring takes time and resources away from the daily operation of the school. Replacing teachers frequently interferes with building a coherent faculty and vision. Teachers do not reach a level of maturity that a school would want from its established staff.

Thus, for these suggestions to become reality, educators must stand up and defend them as necessary aspects of a profession, as characteristics that will improve teaching and learning, eventually benefiting students and society in general. All the players in our public-education system will have to have the will to make these changes. They will not be comfortable. At times they will be messy. There will be setbacks. However, success is in the offing if society understands the potential benefits and is willing to weather the storm of change.

ESSENTIAL IDEAS TO REMEMBER

Members of a profession have an obligation as gatekeepers regarding the training and induction of new members. This includes more preservice time in classrooms for aspiring teachers, and more comprehensive internships lasting at least a full semester.

The cost of high attrition (notorious in education) is high, both in the development of professional resources and the expense of constantly trying to rebuild a faculty.

Cooperating teachers need training (from the sending university) in observation, communication, and specific teaching strategies to perform their jobs well. They should meet as a peer group during the time of the internships, either within the school or with other cooperating teachers across the district. The interns should meet separately as well. There needs to be some sort of compensation for the cooperating teacher (graduate credits, reduced teaching load, salary, or some combination of these). A strong partnership between the school and the university will support substantive and effective internships.

A key aspect of gatekeeping is hiring new members of the profession. Hiring procedures and interview questions should be tied to the school's philosophy. The objective is to hire those individuals who would fit well with the school's belief system, style, and community. Use a teacher committee when hiring. Hiring the right person the first time saves time, money, and trouble.

A profession takes care of its own. In this case, new teacher induction programs can help recent hires acclimate to their new positions and environments. As with internships, the induction program will need something equivalent to the cooperating teacher, in this case the mentor.

Mentors need training. Mentoring is not a political perk, but a real position of responsibility. A school may want to establish support groups for both mentors and mentees. As with cooperating teachers, mentors will need some form of compensation. As with internships, a school–university partnership would be invaluable.

A new-teacher course can facilitate first-year teachers' learning the ropes of their new profession and the specific school system in which they find themselves. This course could include topics such as grading, conducting a parent conference, discipline, district resources and personnel, and special education. The course would be credit-bearing, and the instructor, a local experienced teacher, would be compensated.

Another aspect of induction is community. New teachers are often new residents of the area. They will need practical information about the town, such as where and when to register to vote. They will want to know how to access personal services, such as getting a haircut or buying groceries. This would be a good activity to combine with a luncheon for new teachers and their mentors.

These ideas are doable. All members of the system need to understand the benefits of these ideas. This will be for the professionals to explain to the public, including local politicians and the school board. Then, there must be the will to see these changes through, despite some costs, both personal and financial, setbacks, and opponents. If the will is there, the changes can be successful, thus greatly enhancing the profession and the local school system.

REFERENCES

Danielson, Charlotte. (1996). *Enhancing Professional Practice: A Framework for Teaching.* Alexandria, VA: Association for Supervision and Curriculum Development.

Gardner, H., M. Csikszentmihalyi, and W. Damon (2001). *Good Work.* New York: Basic Books.

Heller, Daniel A. (2004). *Teachers Wanted: Attracting and Retaining Good Teachers.* Alexandria, VA: Association for Supervision and Curriculum Development.

SEVEN

The Product: The Purpose of Public Education

A TRICKY QUESTION

Why do parents bother to send their children to public school? What is the purpose of education? At first, these would seem to be simple questions. However, there are a number of potential answers, and some may be mutually exclusive. Among the responses one will hear are to prepare students to take productive roles as citizens of a democracy, to prepare students for employment, to prepare students for college, to inculcate students with the predominant values of American culture.

There may also be insidious purposes for public education. Do schools perpetuate the socioeconomic divides that now exist in America? Are certain elements of society overrepresented in remedial classes, math and science classes, Advanced Placement (AP) classes? If so, why is this? What society claims as the purpose of education and the actual results of education may not be the same.

EDUCATION AND DEMOCRACY

Clearly, a true democracy relies on an educated and discriminating populace. People need to know how to analyze an argument, to understand complicated situations, and to produce thoughtful responses in the debate of major issues. Voters must be able to communicate clearly and without fear of reprisal for what they say. They must be respectful. They must know how to think.

Do schools teach the basic building blocks for the preservation of democracy? This is debatable. This writer has argued elsewhere that there are four basic skills students should learn in school: kindness, thinking, problem solving, and communication (Heller 2012).

The problems of bullying, harassment, and intimidation cause one to question how effective the schools are in teaching students to be kind to one another. There are now laws demanding that students and teachers treat each other with respect. Why is kindness so important?

Students cannot learn if they are experiencing fear and anxiety, especially when these problems are coming from within the school itself. How can students listen carefully and respond thoughtfully if they are afraid that their comments will be met with derision? They need to feel secure in their membership in the world of free-flowing ideas in order to learn well and participate in the debates of public issues as required in a democracy.

Without mutual respect, conversation breaks down, and the result is what one sees happening in Congress now. Each side offers a position that it feels is mutually exclusive of any other position. There is no actual debate. People need to be open to many ideas and sides of an issue in order to take the best from every position to develop the most useful solution.

In order to discuss issues intelligently, people need to know how to think. Members of the populace have to be able to analyze an issue and construct counterarguments and suggestions. They have to understand the logical consequences of each possibility, including unanticipated consequences. Thinking through an issue or a problem is more than just keeping the thought in one's mind. The individual has to do something with that idea.

This leads to the skill of problem solving. A person thinks through an issue in order to develop a solution to that problem. All the analysis and synthesis of ideas should lead to something, a constructive way to deal with the issue under consideration. People can process an idea forever, so at some point they need to know how to build all the ideas into a structure, or solution with which to meet the needs of the problem at hand.

Finally, without the skill of communication, people will not be able to share their ideas, either as presenters or listeners. Language has to be clear, concise, and unambiguous. It has to be free of invective. It cannot be loaded with jargon and complex structures that block easy understanding.

All of this begs the question: do America's schools prepare students to take their place as productive, responsible citizens of a democracy and of a complex, interactive world of many nations? Gridlock in Congress, poverty, and corporate greed would argue that the nation's schools, and society in general, are not doing so well in this area.

THE GREAT LEVELERS OF SOCIETY

One might think that schools are the great levelers of society. Why else would so many autocratic regimes deny good educations to so many of their citizens? Education allows people the opportunity to know, to understand, and to compete with others in a society. Education is freedom. Education is power. This can be frightening to people who want to hold wealth and power in an exclusive group.

Once again, one has to question whether or not our schools are indeed reaching this goal of political and economic empowerment. Does the education system offer an equal chance to every student, regardless of that student's economic or social class, regardless of where that student comes from or the native language she speaks? These are seriously debatable issues that America has to address.

If schools are the great levelers of society, then there must be explanations for several apparent contradictions. Why do schools in impoverished communities persist in graduating students who are ill prepared? Why do schools composed of primarily minority students persist in graduating kids who are ill prepared? Why are minorities overrepresented in remedial and special education classes? Why are women underrepresented in upper-level math and science classes? Why are minorities underrepresented in AP courses?

WOMEN AND THE PUBLIC SCHOOLS

Women earn only 26 percent of degrees in STEM (science, technology, engineering, and mathematics) related areas (Ramirez 2013, 1). Apparently, women are just as talented as men in math and science, but "the gender gap is caused by attitudes and behaviors toward girls and women, especially in the classroom" (Ramirez 2013). Women's lack of talent in these subjects has become an accepted societal belief.

Many high-school girls see mathematicians as nerds, social outcasts, and loners. Research shows that girls and girls of color take more science courses if they experience more hands-on and fun activities and if they know that someone will keep working with them until all of them understand the answers to all of their questions (National Engineers Week Foundation 2013, 6). Furthermore, "Don't assume teachers are aware that most current practices discourage girls in math and science" (National Engineers Week Foundation 2013, 7).

Consequently, American schools are perpetuating attitudes that deter girls from taking more math and science courses and choosing college majors that lead to careers in these fields. As former Yale associate professor Ainissa Ramirez (2013) says,

> The 21st century requires a new kind of learner—not someone who can simply churn out answers by rote, but a student who can think expansively and solve problems resourcefully. As a scientist and inventor, a longtime professor at Yale University, and a woman who has always been passionate about getting kids passionate about science, I believe that the key to this goal is to improve science, technology, and engineering and math (STEM) education. These disciplines are rooted in the kind of thinking that is now critical. One of the most important aspects of this shift is to fix the false presumption that girls are not as good as boys in science and math. (1)

It is time for America's schools to encourage all students in the STEM areas, not just some, through innovations in pedagogy that appeal to girls and providing positive models of achievement and success for all genders, races, and socioeconomic levels.

THE ISSUE OF MINORITIES

Another area of concern is the underrepresentation of minorities in AP classes. In 2012, 32.4 percent of graduating high-school students took one or more AP exams. However, looking at students deemed likely to pass one of these prestigious tests, the percentage of African Americans signing up for the test drops to 20 percent, Hispanics to 30 percent, and Native Americans to 20 percent. The percentage for whites was 40, and for Asian and Pacific Islanders 60 (Brown 2013, 1).

There is a similar underrepresentation of minorities as opposed to whites in gifted and talented programs. This can be attributed to "cross-cultural misunderstanding, assessment bias, and teacher referral processes" (Mid-Atlantic Equity Center, n.d., 1). Once again, one can trace the problem to the behaviors of the school itself rather than to the students. Whether knowingly or not, some public-school practices hold minority students back from realizing their full potential.

"When it comes to math and science, minority students are 'often not recognized as the smart kids in class,'" says Mary Walker, an education professor at the University of Texas in Austin who focuses on math and science education (Brown 2013, 2). She goes on to say,

> If you don't cultivate students' interest and aptitude for a subject early in their educational careers . . . increasing their access to AP exams may simply be too little too late. ((Brown 2013, 2)

In other words, here is another area in which schools may be failing to maximize the potential of all students, in this case minority students.

In addition to the above issues, minority students are overrepresented in special education classes and in programs for the mentally retarded (Zhang and Katsiyannis 2002, 180). Rates for African Americans in the categories of "all disabilities" and "emotionally behaviorally disturbed" are higher than that for whites (Zhang and Katsiyannis 2002, 182). According to the US Department of Education, African American students make up 16 percent of the student population but make up as much as 32 percent of the population in some special education programs (Zorigian and Job, n.d., 1). These authors claim:

> No evidence exists to show that minority students have innately more exceptionalities than white students, so why is this happening? The answers lie in socioeconomic status and pre-conceived notions of race. (Zorigian and Job, n.d., 2)

A study at the University of Kansas of the disproportionate number of minority students as compared to whites in special education "thus far has shown that racial bias may be an important factor" (Krings 2012, 1). The study goes on to explain that, after desegregation, schools create new more prestigious categories of special education for whites while leaving minorities in the lower-ranked groups, a strategy known as "categorical manipulation"(Krings 2012, 1). Thus, whites in special education remain in a privileged position as compared to minorities in special education.

This can lead to the minority students receiving "low-quality services and watered-down curriculum instead of effective support" (Harvard Graduate School of Education, n.d., 2).

> Despite possibly good intentions, children in special education are most often relegated to learning environments with less rigor, as the focus is often the management of emotional and behavioral issues, learning disabilities and other "impairments" rather than on academic excellence, capacity development or preparing students to participate in the global marketplace. (Codrington and Fairchild 2012, 2)

THE MORE INSIDIOUS SIDE OF PUBLIC EDUCATION

Yet another contributing factor to the overrepresentation of minorities in special education is the hidden curriculum, "the expectations we have of our students that are not explicitly taught . . .drawn from middle-class value systems" (Zorigian and Job n.d., 2). Such values include "raising one's hand before speaking" and "learning to read by being read to at bedtime" (Zorigian and Job n.d., 2).

> When teachers encounter these students in the classroom, they often mistake their lack of knowledge of the hidden curriculum for disabilities or exceptionalities and refer them for special education services, when perhaps direct instruction or some reading remediation would have helped more. (Zorigian and Job n.d., 2)

A more insidious lesson one can extrapolate from this inculcation of middle-class values and practices is that the school actually exists to perpetuate white hegemony. The only values that count are those that maintain majority power and wealth, while other groups of people are shunted off into more restrictive and limiting programs.

> As long as the behavior, learning style, and ability and achievement levels of African descended children are defined by White constructs of normality, they will continue to be placed into special education at disproportionate rates, which maintains extant power relations. (Codrington and Fairchild 2012, 24)

In addition, according to Codrington and Fairchild (2012, 5), "Restrictive school settings have been a 'warehouse' principally for African American males, which led to continued warehousing in correctional facilities." The authors go so far as to say

> Knowledge is power, as one's potential or abilities in life are maximized with education. Withholding, limiting access to, or decreasing the quality of education has been one of America's built-in racist tendencies against people of African descent and a primary tool of White supremacy. (Codrington and Fairchild 2012, 6)

If one returns to the purpose of education as preparing individuals to take productive places in a democracy, then the above constitutes a truly dangerous and sad situation. It is even worse when one considers that these circumstances may exist for other minorities as well. All of this information begs the question, Does the public education system have, as one of its goals, maintaining the current power and economic situation to the detriment of particular groups of citizens?

PREPARATION FOR THE WORKFORCE

Some people might suggest that the purpose of school is to prepare individuals to enter the workforce successfully and become productive human beings. While this is very likely one purpose of schools, alone it is a reductive one. Doesn't society want more for its youth than for them to be prepared as cogs for the economy and industry? Should not schools also be concerned with students' spiritual and ethical development, about their ability to involve themselves in our democracy, and to become good people able to live the good life?

If preparation for the workforce is a major purpose of education, one might even then question how well the schools perform in this area. Are students well prepared for gainful employment and economic independence? Do they have the necessary skills sought by employers in the twenty-first century? There is evidence that they do not.

In 2006,

> a collaboration [of] The Conference Board, Corporate Voices for Working Families, the Partnership for 21st Century Skills, and the Society for Human Resource Management conducted an in-depth study of the cor-

porate perspective on the readiness of new entrants into the U.S. workforce by level of educational attainment. The study includes results from both an in-depth survey conducted during April and May 2006 and interviews with a sampling of a dozen HR and other senior executives. (Conference Board, Inc., the Partnership for 21st Century Skills, Corporate Voices for Working Families, and the Society for Human Resource Management 2006, 2)

This report clearly designates what skills employers seek, and their satisfaction with job candidates with respect to these skills. While the study is divided into three categories of potential employees (high-school graduates, two-year college graduates, and four-year graduates), this chapter concerns itself only with high-school graduates, since the topic here is the purpose of America's public schools.

The study reflects interviews with over four hundred employers across the United States (Conference Board, Inc., the Partnership for 21st Century Skills, Corporate Voices for Working Families, and the Society for Human Resource Management 2006, 9). For high-school students, the top five basic knowledge skills employers sought were as follows:

> *Reading Comprehension (in English)* with nearly two-thirds (62.5 percent) of employer respondents rating this skill as "very important," followed by *English Language (spoken)* (61.8 percent), *Writing in English* (49.4 percent), *Mathematics* (30.4 percent), and *Foreign Languages* (11.0 percent). Knowledge of *Science* is close behind *Foreign Languages* with 9.0 percent saying *Science* is "very important" for high school graduates. (Conference Board, Inc., the Partnership for 21st Century Skills, Corporate Voices for Working Families, and the Society for Human Resource Management 2006, 18)

In addition, the five most important applied skills for high-school graduates as potential employees were as follows:

> *Professionalism/Work Ethic* (80.3 percent), *Teamwork/Collaboration* (74.7 percent), *Oral Communications* (70.3 percent), *Ethics/Social Responsibility* (63.4 percent), and *Critical Thinking/Problem Solving* (57.5 percent). (Conference Board, Inc., the Partnership for 21st Century Skills, Corporate Voices for Working Families, and the Society for Human Resource Management 2006, 20)

According to the report, 42 percent of employers rated the overall preparation of high-school graduates for the entry-level jobs they fill as "deficient" across the country regardless of the type of industry examined (Conference Board, Inc., the Partnership for 21st Century Skills, Corporate Voices for Working Families, and the Society for Human Resource Management 2006, 31). Among those areas considered by employers to be most deficient were Writing in English (72 percent) and Math (53.5 percent). Even such skills as the English Language and Reading Comprehension were rated as merely adequate by 73.1 percent and 58.2 percent of employers, respectively (Conference Board, Inc., the Partnership for 21st Century Skills, Corporate Voices for Working Families, and the Society for Human Resource Management 2006, 32).

With respect to applied skills the situation was worse. Among those skills in which high school graduates were considered deficient were Written Composition (80.9 percent), Professionalism/Work Ethic (70.3 percent), Critical Thinking/Problem Solving (69.6 percent), and Lifelong Learning/Self-Direction (58.2 percent) (Conference Board, Inc., the Partnership for 21st Century Skills, Corporate Voices for Working Families, and the Society for Human Resource Management 2006, 32).

One can only assume, according to these findings, that employers see the American public-education system doing a poor job in preparing students for the workplace. Consequently, if this is the purpose of public schools, they are fulfilling it poorly. In conclusion,

> Surveys consistently show that many high school graduates do not meet employers' standards in a variety of academic areas, as well as in employability skills such as attendance, teamwork and collaboration, and work habits. (Bangser 2008, 4)

PREPARATION FOR POSTSECONDARY EDUCATION

This naturally leads to an examination of the final possible purpose of K–12 public education: to prepare students for successful entry into postsecondary education.

While this purpose is somewhat limited, it suggests a richer future for students than merely preparing for the workforce. Here again, though, there is the question of whether or not public education actually achieves this goal. A *Washington Times* article begins, "The vast majority of the nation's 2012 high school students aren't ready for college, and SAT [Scholastic Aptitude Test] reading scores have plummeted to their lowest level in four decades (Wolfgang 2012, 1). The author goes on to say that 57 percent of students taking the test failed to reach the test's benchmark for college and career readiness, 1550 points out of 1600. Attaining the benchmark gives students a good chance at earning a B- or better average during their first year of college (Wolfgang 2012, 1).

In 2011, only 28 percent of students taking the ACT (American College Testing) qualified as college ready in all four core subject areas. In addition, there remained significant gaps between various racial and ethnic groups (Clairborne 2011, 1). White or Asian American students had the best scores in English, Reading, Math, and Science, while African Americans had the lowest, with Latinos being the next best group (Clairborne 2011, 1–2).

> Readiness was defined as having a 50 percent chance of getting a B or a 75 percent chance of getting a C in first-year courses English Composition, College Algebra, Biology, and social sciences. (Clairborne, 2011, 2)

An article in *Education Week*, reappearing in the Hechinger Report, went into further detail on the problem with student readiness for postsecondary education. In 2013, the composite ACT score dropped to 20.9, resulting in the lowest scores in eight years (Adams 2013, 1).

According to the Southern Regional Education Board and the National Center for Public Policy and Higher Education, nearly 60 percent of first-year college students are not adequately prepared for college-level work, even though they have met all the entry requirements necessary for gaining admittance to college. These students found that they had to take remedial courses in English or Math (NCPPHE and SREB 2010, 1). "Their high school diploma, college preparatory curriculum, and high school exit examination scores did not ensure college readiness" (NCPPHE and SREB 2010, 1).

This report elaborates several reasons for this gap in college readiness. For instance, high-school diplomas do not guarantee readiness, nor do high-stakes exit exams.

> Earning a high school diploma does not mean that graduates are ready for college. Most states that have high school exit exams or other "high-stakes" tests readily acknowledge that the exams measure proficiency at the 8th- to 10th-grade levels. (NCPPHE and SREB 2010, 3)

Other sources of poor preparation include college prep curricula that fail to teach critical thinking and the fact that K–12 educational goals and postsecondary institution entry-level skills are set independently of one another. There is no guarantee that taking courses and fulfilling seat-time expectations will result in the skills necessary for college success. Traditional standardized tests may not measure college readiness adequately. Schools and teachers are not being held to a standard of ensuring college readiness in students. Colleges do not take responsibility for degree completion (NCPPHE and SREB 2010, 3–6).

K–12 public school systems and colleges need to work together to ensure success.

> Finally, current efforts in the states to strengthen college readiness do not fully recognize the need to make P–12 and postsecondary education equal partners in the readiness agenda. Many states still view the lack of college readiness as a problem best addressed by P–12 schools. For a high school course of study to yield college-ready graduates, however, both P–12 and postsecondary education must be in complete agreement about explicit readiness standards. Moreover, the two sectors must have a shared stake in success, as measured by the share of high school graduates enrolling directly in and succeeding at college-level courses. Without a shared stake, post-secondary institutions can

use lack of readiness as an excuse for their own low graduation rates. Currently, no state accountability system provides incentives for the two sectors to work together to deliver these outcomes. (NCPPHE and SREB 2010, 7)

Too often politics and public pressures guide state standards, preferring that they be attainable enough for most students to reach, and thus keep constituencies happy, rather than setting the bar at actual college-readiness levels.

Another study revealed that college instructors are well aware of the lack of readiness of their students. In fact, "only 26 percent of college faculty think students are ready" (O'Shaughnessy 2013, 1). This again points to the lack of alignment between high school and college definitions of college readiness (O'Shaughnessy 2013, 1). This situation is further aggravated by high-school grade inflation.

> While college professors complain that many students are unprepared for the rigors of college work, high school grade point averages have steadily climbed. According to the U.S. Department of Education, the average grade point average for male and female high school students is 3.1 and 2.9, respectively. That has risen steadily over the years. In 1990 boys had an average GPA of 2.59 and girls averaged 2.77.
>
> Tellingly, however, while GPA's have increased significantly, ACT and SAT scores have not. This suggests grade inflation is behind the rise in GPA. (O'Shaughnessy 2013, 2)

Consequently, Americans must question this goal of college readiness. If this is a goal of the educational system, then why are the schools failing to comply with it, and in fact increasing the gap through grade inflation? Either the schools have goals that they do not meet, which are not really goals, or they maintain the current power and economic structure to the benefit of some and the disadvantage of others. Neither of these possibilities is a comfortable one.

THE GOOD LIFE

Ideally, the purpose of public school would be to prepare each student for actively engaging in the good life. It is not enough to be college ready or workplace ready. Schools should help students to be whole people: intellectually, spiritually, morally, physically, artistically, and economically. No one should forget the arts or the importance of living a healthy lifestyle. Whole people are able to engage in and enjoy all the aspects of what it means to be a human being. Anything less is reductive at best and cynical at worst.

Do Americans have the political will and honesty to examine the public schools to determine what their mission is and what it should be? Do they have the moral courage to look directly at what is happening? Even then, one can legitimately question whether or not the schools are reaching those ends that Americans say are the purpose of education.

Rather than simply testing students to see if their schools are operating as they should, can Americans see a broader purpose of the schools as an integral and crucial vehicle for the development of purposeful beings prepared to fully engage in the life of the mind and body in a democratic society?

To do this will take some hard work and honesty. America cannot allow its schools simply to churn out cogs for an economic system. It cannot do nothing more than prepare students for further schooling. All students must be prepared for life, to be lifelong learners, and to be on the road to self-actualization. They must all have the same opportunities despite their various backgrounds. Then, and only then, will America's schools be doing justice to democracy and the fullest value of life.

ESSENTIAL IDEAS TO REMEMBER

Determining the purpose of America's public schools is not as simple as it appears. There are a number of possible answers to the question, and some are actually undesirable. Among the possibilities are preparation for participation in a democratic society, leveling society so that everyone has equal opportunities, preparation for the workplace, preparation for postsecondary education, and preparation for living the good life as whole human beings.

In terms of preparing students for life in a democracy, schools should be teaching in four primary areas: kindness, thinking, problem-solving, and communication. Various aspects of human behavior in America suggest that the schools are not doing a very good job at this.

One can question whether or not schools are leveling society. Women remain underrepresented in math and science programs. Various minorities, especially African Americans, are overrepresented in special education and underrepresented in AP courses. This also applies to differences in the opportunities for low- and high-socioeconomic-level students. In fact, one of the hidden purposes of the schools may in fact be to maintain current power and economic divisions among various social groups.

Some say that schools should primarily be preparing students for entry into the workforce. Besides this goal being somewhat limited and reductive, evidence indicates that the educational system is not doing a very good job of this.

Similarly, others say that the main purpose of public schools is to prepare students for postsecondary education. Again, one can see this goal as reductive. In addition, as with preparation for the workforce, the schools' achievement of this goal is definitely questionable.

Finally, Americans should want more for their children, beyond all of the goals discussed above. Schools should be preparing students for life in a democracy, readiness for the workforce, and readiness for postsecondary education. In addition to this, however, the schools should be helping students to become whole human beings, on their way to being self-actualized. This would include working in all areas of human development. Schools should help students to be whole people: intellectually, spiritually, morally, physically, artistically, and economically.

REFERENCES

Adams, Caralee. (August 21, 2013). "Most Students Aren't Ready for College, ACT Data Show." Hechinger Report/*Education Week*. http://hechingerreport.org/most-students-arent-ready-for-college-act-data-show_12951/.

Bangser, Michael. (2008). "Preparing High School Students for Successful Transitions to Postsecondary Education and Employment." National High School Issue Brief. http://www.betterhighschools.org/docs/PreparingHSStudentsforTransition_073108.pdf.

Brown, Ryan Lenora. (February 20, 2013). "Why Promising Minority Students Aren't Signing Up for AP Exams." *Christian Science Monitor*. http://www.csmonitor.com/USA/Education/2013/0220/Why-promising-minority-students-aren-t-signing-up-for-AP-exams.

Clairborne, Ron. (August 17, 2011). "College-Bound Students Not Prepared in Basic Subjects." ABC News via World News. http://abcnews.go.com/US/majority-college-bound-students-qualified/story?id=14325199.

Codrington, Jamila, and Halford H. Fairchild. (2012). "Special Education and Miseducation of African American Children: A Call to Action." Association of Black Psychologists. www.abpsi.org.

Conference Board, Inc., Partnership for 21st Century Skills, Corporate Voices for Working Families, and Society for Human Resource Management. (2006). *Are They Really Ready to Work? Employers' Perspectives on the Basic Knowledge and Applied Skills of New Entrants to the 21st Century U.S. Workforce*. http://www.p21.org/storage/documents/FINAL_REPORT_PDF09-29-06.pdf.

Harvard Graduate School of Education. (n.d.). "Harvard Studies Find Inappropriate Special Education Placements Continue to Segregate and Limit Educational Opportunities for Minority Students Nationwide." http://www.gse.harvard.edu/news_events/featiures/2001/speced03022001.html.

Heller, Daniel A. 2012. *Curriculum on the Edge of Survival: How Schools Fail to Prepare Students for Membership in a Democracy*, 2nd ed. Lanham, MD: Rowman and Littlefield.

Krings, Mike. (July 23, 2012). "Study Shows Race Played a Role in Placing Minorities in Special Education Categories." KU News Service. http://achive.news.ku.edu/2012/july23/specialeducationstudy.shtml.

Mid-Atlantic Equity Center. (n.d.). "The Over-Representation and Under-Representation of Minority Students in Special Education and Gifted and Talented Programs." MAEC at the George Washington University Center for Equity and Excellence in Education. http://maec.ceee.gwu.edu/appropriate-representation-low-income-and-minority-students-special-education-and-gifted-and-talented.

National Center for Public Policy and Higher Education and Southern Regional Education Board (NCPPHE and SREB). (2010). "Beyond the Rhetoric: Improving College Readiness through Coherent State Policy." http://www.highereducation.org/reports/college_readiness/gap/shtm.

National Engineers Week Foundation. (February 21, 2013). "Introduce a Girl to Engineering Day." http://www.eweek.org/site/News/Eweek/girlsdayinfo.shtml.

O'Shaughnessy, Lynn. (April 19, 2013). "Is Your 'A' Student Really Ready for College?" Money Watch/CBS News. http://cbsnews.com/8301-505145_162-57580233/is-your-a-student-really-ready-for-college/.

Ramirez, Ainissa. (January 31, 2013). "Girls and Science: A Dream Deferred" [Web log post]. http://www.edutopia.org/blog/girls-and-science-dream-deferred.

Wolfgang, Ben. (September 24, 2012). "Data: High School Students Aren't Ready for College." *Washington Times.* http://www.washingtontimes.com/news/2012/sep/24/high-school-grads-reading-skills-hit-new-low-most-/?page=all.

Zhang, Dalun, and Antonis Katsiyannis. (May/June 2002). "Minority Representation in Special Education: A Persistent Challenge." *Remedial and Special Education* 23, no. 3: (180–87). Hammil Institute of Disabilities and Sage Publications. http://www.rse.sagepub.com/cgi/content/abstract/23/3/180Minority.

Zorigian, Kris, and Jennifer Job. (n.d.). "Representation in Special Education Classrooms." LEARN NC. University of North Carolina at Chapel Hill School of Education. http://www.learnnc.org/lp/pages/6799.

Conclusion

The chapters in this book cover a broad range of issues concerning the public education system in America. Yet, there is much overlap. How can schools recapture potential dropouts before they leave unless the schools are structured in new ways? How can schools serve a wider range of students without new delivery systems?

How can teachers become professionals without a new governance system in education? How can schools fulfill their missions without first being clear on their purpose? How will schools improve without better preservice and induction programs for new and aspiring teachers? How will all of these changes be possible without people being patient and kind?

The changes proposed in this book range from simple to extraordinarily complex. One wonders how any of this can be done. If schools were factories, we would close them down, retool, test the new systems, and then reopen for production. But schools are not factories, and closing them down as we refit them is not an option.

What we have done in the past is to apply patches to fix schools. If there is a problem, introduce a new program, a new law, a new procedure. By this time, we are applying patches to patches. We need to retool, to build the system anew, rather than continue piecemeal approaches to improving our schools. We need to rethink how we, as a nation, do education.

Perhaps we can develop a transition process by which a few schools at a time are discontinued and replaced with new schools that reflect the changes suggested. Then the process of education could continue as the improved schools come on line. Think of a new power plant. While it is being built, power continues to flow to the public from already existing plants. When it is complete, with all the latest innovation, it can go online and the older plant can shut down.

Attitudes will have to change. Agreeing to innovation on the condition that one's own part to play does not change will not work. There is too much vested interest in doing things the way they have always been done. Individuals naturally want to hold on to what they have, their traditions, patterns, and power. Players from the federal government to the local school boards to the teachers, parents, and students must accept new roles and relationships for change to happen.

America has always been able to get the job done. Citizens have been willing to sacrifice during wartime, such as World War II. They made do with what they had, women took over what were traditionally men's jobs, and men learned new skills in the armed forces. We sent a man to the moon. We have eradicated once deadly and threatening diseases. Why can't we meet the challenge of rethinking our education system?

There were funds and other resources for the accomplishments mentioned above. They required massive coordination of parts and subsystems. How is this different from rebuilding our schools?

There is a serious lack of trust in teachers and schools. Educators should be allowed to make educational decisions, while lay boards and federal, state, and local governments concern themselves with the broad strokes of education policy, not the day-to-day operation of schools. Others besides schools need to step up to the plate in the endeavor to deal with social issues such as violence, apathy, interpersonal relationships, and drugs.

Other public servants, such as firefighters and police officers, are left to do their jobs, even though they, like teachers, are paid through taxes on the community. Why can we not allow teachers and principals to do their jobs without trying to control everything that occurs or to constantly second-guess the decisions these people make? It is time to elevate teaching to the professional status it deserves.

Besides trust and necessary resources, there will be change and sacrifice if we are to make our educational system the best it can be. This takes political will. We have to decide to go all in, to do the job, regardless of how long it takes, how much it costs, or how much temporary disruption it causes.

Can we muster the patience, the energy, and the commitment to make it happen? There will be many false starts, failed attempts, and long conversations along the way. If we will not move unless we have a guarantee of success, then we might as well not even start. We will have to have a high tolerance for ambiguity and the uncertainty that come with major change.

The old *Nation at Risk* report published during the Reagan administration claimed that if another country forced the educational system we had on us, we would consider it an act of war. Strong words for an overwhelming challenge. We can meet this challenge, as we have met numerous challenges in the past. We simply have to decide that we are going to do it, not for political reasons, not for control issues, but for our children and the future of America.

The issue of public education in a democratic society cuts across all socioeconomic levels, political parties, races and ethnicities, and cultural differences. We need schools that serve all possible students, helping them to become whole human beings. When we can do that, then we can say that we are finished, that the schools are in good shape, that the schools work.

Until then, we have to exert the necessary will and resources for making fundamental changes in the way schools work and the way they are run. Until we make the commitment, the schools will flounder, teachers will still not be true professionals, and society's inequities will remain. Once change is under way, we must suspend disbelief, remain flexible, and remember that we are committing to a cause that is bigger than any one individual.

It will be a long journey.

About the Author

Daniel Heller has been an educator since 1975. He holds both a BA and MA in English from Middlebury College in Vermont, an MEd in curriculum and instruction from Keene (New Hampshire) State College, and a certificate of advanced graduate studies in educational administration and planning from the University of Vermont. In addition, he holds an honorary Doctor of Humanities degree from the College of St. Joseph in Rutland, Vermont. Besides teaching, Dan has served as a department head, director of professional development, principal, and curriculum coordinator. He has presented on educational topics throughout the United States and in Canada and China. His other books include *Teachers Wanted: Attracting and Retaining Good Teachers* (2004), *Curriculum on the Edge of Survival: How Schools Fail to Prepare Students for Membership in a Democracy* (2012), and *Taoist Lessons for Educational Leaders: Gentle Pathways to Resolving Conflicts* (2012). He has also published numerous articles, chapters, and columns for the Association for Supervision and Curriculum Development, Phi Delta Kappa, the National Council of Teachers of English, and others. He has spent most of his career in Vermont, where he lives with his wife of thirty-eight years, Nina. He can be reached at helrdan1@gmail.com.